Thorstein Veblen

Thorstein Veblen, ca. 1907

Thorstein Veblen

The Carleton College Veblen Seminar Essays

Edited by

Carlton C. Qualey

Columbia University Press

New York & London

1968

The photograph of Thorstein Veblen which serves as the frontispiece of this book is reproduced by permission of the owner, Mr. R. L. Duffus of Palo Alto, California. The photographer is unknown.

To the Veblen Seminar Students

Robert H. Alsdorf
Robert J. Bremer
Peter A. Butzin
Catherine M. Covey
Dorothy A. Dahlenburg
Harry G. Fuller
Frederick S. Harrod
Mary Lou Hoerr
Lynn A. Hunt
Peter J. Iverson
David M. Mindock
John R. Myer
Susan Palmer
Richard L. Sadler
Joanne C. Wakeland

Preface

IN RECOGNITION of the centennial year of Carleton College in Northfield, Minnesota, it seemed appropriate to its faculty committee administering the Fred C. Andersen Foundation in American Studies to approve as the theme of the fall 1966 American Studies Seminar the ideas and significance of the college's celebrated and perhaps most significant alumnus, Thorstein Bunde Veblen of the class of 1880. Thanks to the Andersen Foundation it was possible to invite six distinguished scholars to participate in as many sessions of the ten-week seminar. The seminar was composed of fifteen senior students, six women and nine men, selected from the large number of applicants and representing several major fields of study. From this seminar came the essays published in this book and fifteen student papers, the latter subsequently judged by a Veblen authority as being of graduate quality. It was found impracticable to include the student essays, totaling 485 pages of manuscript, in the book, but they may be examined in bound form in the library of Carleton College. During the summer preceding the seminar the students were required to read most of the Veblen books and also David M. Potter's *People of Plenty* and John Kenneth Galbraith's *The Affluent Society.** I served as director of the seminar.

The general approach of the seminar was to Veblen as a

* David M. Potter, *People of Plenty, Economic Abundance and the American Character* (Chicago, University of Chicago Press, 1954) ; John Kenneth Galbraith, *The Affluent Society* (Boston, Houghton Mifflin, 1958).

major social critic. The emphasis was on the relevance of Veblen for America of the 1960s. It would be fair to say that a greater relevance was found than anyone had anticipated, despite the great changes in American society since his lifetime. It would have comforted the seminar to have had the opportunity to read the new book by John Kenneth Galbraith, *The New Industrial State,* published subsequently, in which he writes:

Power has, in fact, passed to what anyone in search of novelty might be justified in calling a new factor of production. This is the association of men of diverse technical knowledge, experience or other talent which modern industrial technology and planning require. It extends from the leadership of the modern industrial enterprise down to just short of the labor force and embraces a large number of people and a large variety of talent.*

Of course Galbraith's analysis of modern society is not the same as Veblen's, but it is interesting to note the "machine process" still very much alive in contemporary analyses.

In addition to the machine process, the seminar examined Veblen's concept of the pecuniary culture, the separation of ownership and control, the nature of private property, absentee ownership, conspicuous consumption, industrial sabotage, the captain of industry concept, Veblen's technician in society, his treatment of salesmanship, the important instinct psychology, the role of myths, the place of higher education, the factor of patriotism, and the relation of the machine process to the modern dynastic state. As evidenced by the extensive bibliographies in the student essays, very little relevant material would seem to have been overlooked. It was the unanimous feeling of the seminar participants, including its

* Galbraith, *The New Industrial State* (Boston, Houghton Mifflin, 1967), pp. 58–59.

director, that America of the 1960s would benefit greatly from the social criticism of another Veblen.

The thanks of the editor and publisher for permissions to quote go to Houghton Mifflin Company (John Kenneth Galbraith, *The New Industrial State*) ; D. Van Nostrand Company (Thomas C. Cochran, *Basic History of American Business* [Anvil 39], copyright 1959) ; Harper and Row (Mircea Eliade, *The Sacred and the Profane*) ; and Augustus M. Kelley Publishers (Joseph Dorfman, *Thorstein Veblen and His America,* reprint edition) .

It is a pleasure to acknowledge the assistance of those directly involved in the publication of this book. Thanks go first to the Fred C. Andersen Foundation in American Studies which made the book possible. The essayists represented gave generously of their time and energy during their visits to the Carleton College campus, and it was a great pleasure and privilege to have them participate in the seminar. Thanks go also to the fifteen students who made the seminar a memorable experience. To them this book is dedicated. I am especially grateful for the advice and counsel of Professor Joseph Dorfman of Columbia University, and the appreciation of all concerned goes to the able staff of the Columbia University Press. What Veblen himself would have said about this enterprise is almost unimaginable.

C.C.Q.

February, 1968

Contents

Thorstein Veblen

Introduction

Carlton C. Qualey

Change and development there were in Veblen's ideas, but his guide lines remained always those of a sophisticated, sceptical, Norwegian agrarian thrown into contact with the impersonal calculus of the profit economy as it took form in modern corporation finance.[1]

He was a man living in a shell formed by long years of alienation and hurt, and perhaps also by the glimpses of terror he had when he probed into the nature of institutions and the course of history.[2]

In his retreat among the lovely coast hills of California, he died on August 3, 1929, a "placid unbeliever" to the end.[3]

I

THE SEVENTY-TWO YEARS from July 30, 1857, until his death form for the student of the life and thought of Thorstein Bunde Veblen the record of an extraordinary mind. The owner of this mind was born into a Norwegian immigrant family, struggled through the handicaps of an inferior basic education and a limited undergraduate training, and found real challenge only when he met students with minds of equivalent capacity at Johns Hopkins and Yale. That he turned to social criticism rather than follow the direction of his graduate field, philosophy, has had various explanations.

He was certainly in the company of a great many who were
doing the same thing toward the end of the nineteenth century and the early part of the twentieth. Henry George,
Edward Bellamy, Brooks and Henry Adams, Frederick Jackson Turner, Lester Ward, John Dewey, John R. Commons,
and a host of others were all disturbed by what seemed to
them a national loss of an earlier virtue and a tendency
toward economic inequality, with its consequent threat to
American democracy. Among intellectuals of the time the
concern amounted to a consensus. Veblen was more representative than unusual in this interest. Why he stood out
from all the rest and why he survived to be quoted more than
others was the problem that faced the Veblen Seminar at
Carleton College in the fall of 1966. In this introduction an
attempt will be made to summarize what the seminar found
and concluded, but with inevitable injection of the editor's
own interpretations, especially in the first section. For the
remainder of the book, the essayists will speak for themselves.

It has been repeatedly asserted that Veblen had a peculiar
animus toward the capitalistic society he found in the United
States, and that this animus was derived in considerable
measure from his Norwegian background. It is interesting to
note that his close friend and associate, Isador Lubin, in
seminar discussion, firmly asserted that Veblen had no such
animus, that he was in fact rather bourgeois in tastes, and
that his interest was purely analytical. Be that as it may,
there is no question as to the importance of his Norwegian
inheritance and of his persistent reverence for it.

There is no need here to repeat Joseph Dorfman's meticu-
lous tracing of the Veblen family's origins. Because of the
manifestly strong influence of Veblen's father on him, at issue

is whether or not the father communicated to Veblen the farmer's suspicion of the official and business classes of Norway. Was this animus carried with the father to the United States, was it reflected as status achieving in the name change, and did it show up in his life in the Nerstrand, Minnesota, farming community? Veblen's brother, Andrew, whose career was also a distinguished one, challenged the view that Veblen's father had any special animus because of his status as a tenant farmer in Norway.[4] The comparative status of a freeholder and a tenant farmer varied considerably in nineteenth-century Norway. The difference might be wide, as between a large farmer and a poor cotter, or it might be narrow or even reversed in emphasis as between a debt-ridden freeholder and a prosperous tenant who rented one or more farms and who in turn sublet land. According to Andrew, the father was in the latter category and never regarded himself as being of an inferior status. The problem of name-changing is a common one. In the strict sense only a freeholder could use the place name as a family name, but in practice the place name was widely used. The alternative was the familiar custom of using the father's first name and adding "son," that is, Peterson, Johnson, Oleson. Although Veblen's father did use the name Anderson in registration of land title in his first Wisconsin land contracts, he resumed the Veblen name in such contracts when he moved to Minnesota. It is Andrew Veblen's contention that his father never ceased to use the Veblen name, and that no implications of status building or inferiority can be read into the name change. It would appear that little is to be gained by emphasizing either the leasehold or name status as a source, via his father, of Veblen's attitudes toward the business classes.

Mention has been made of Veblen's self-consciousness (the

outsider syndrome) about his English language deficiency
when he went to Northfield (Minnesota) Academy. His
brother Andrew vehemently stated that Thorstein knew English well before he attended the school, and that he had no
sense of being a "Norskie" in a New England type school.[5] In
fact, several of the Veblen children attended this school, all
presumably equally handicapped. Veblen learned languages
easily and mastered several later. This source of Veblen's
"animus" can also be discounted.

More significant is Veblen's lifelong veneration of the pre-
Christian Viking heritage. A project started during his years
of unemployment in the 1880s, and completed late in life,
was a translation of the *Laxdaela Saga*.[6] This tale of blood
feuds in Norway and Iceland seems to have had a special
attractiveness for Veblen. What he admired especially was the
toughness of the family, the simple economic unit, composed
of farmers-traders-hunters-raiders-colonizers-innovators-crafts-
men. Into this basic, obviously idealized, natural society came
the infusion of "business" interests in the competition
for lands and trade by family heads. Competition led to the
famous blood feuds, which in turn brought impoverishment
and slavery. The ultimate sanctification of this economic system by the Roman Catholic Church, involving acceptance of
lot and subservience, caused Veblen in his introduction to
say:

The subsequent share of the Holy Church and its clerics in the
ulterior degradation of the Scandinavian peoples, including Iceland,
was something incredibly shameful and shabby. . . . The medieval
Church in Iceland stands out in the current of events as a corporation of bigoted adventurers for the capitalizing of graft and black-
mail and the profitable compounding of felonious crimes and
vices.[7]

If there was any documentary basis for Veblen's original economic Eden, as in David Noble's essay, it was the Scandinavian Viking family unit of the pre-Christian era.

Veblen did not come from an impoverished or underprivileged home. His father, Thomas, was a successful farmer, by any standard, both in his first enterprises in Wisconsin and certainly in the Nerstrand community, in Minnesota. The Veblen children were tutored at home and later went to both the traditional Norwegian Lutheran summer school and the regular term English school "west of the [Valley] Grove [Woods]." [8] Seven of the children attended Carleton, either in the academy or the college.

The Nerstrand farms were in units of ninety and two hundred acres of good farming land and woods. The farm home that was ultimately constructed by the father, according to his own design, is still standing, an unusually well-designed home both for those days and ours. There is no evidence of poverty despite the large family and the support of hired help. As Joseph Dorfman has shown, what Thorstein admired and enjoyed was the use of the new mechanical devices and inventions that were coming into the market. Although the family was Lutheran, it is clear that it was not dogmatically so. The choice of the Yankee school rather than the Lutheran school in nearby Northfield is evidence of an independent mind, although the parents did not need to be concerned with the soundness of Christian doctrine as taught in the fledgling Congregational Northfield Academy.

What one senses from the memoirs of Thorstein's sister Emily, and from his brother Andrew's statements, is an unmistakable pride of family status. The loyalty of the family to its members is clear, especially in the sustained support of

Thorstein through his years of unemployment, after he had won his doctorate at Yale. The large headstone in the Valley Grove Cemetery in Nerstrand proudly identifies the last resting place of the Veblens. This was no ordinary family, even among Norwegian settlers.

When Thorstein came to Northfield Academy, in 1874, and after three years entered Carleton College he came not as an inferior but as a Veblen. The imprint of his parents' intellectual vigor and stamina was indelible on Thorstein, as it was also on Andrew, Emily, and the others who attended the same school. Much has been made of his idiosyncrasies of behavior, but the fact remains that Thorstein was allowed to complete the college course in three years (1877–1880), an indication of genuine respect. John Bates Clark, as Dorfman so well demonstrates, was for Veblen the most stimulating teacher at Carleton College, and it is possible that Clark's teaching had something to do with Veblen's ultimate choice of field for writing and teaching. At the time, Veblen's interest was in philosophy.

The evidence of his family associations and his school and college experience shows a precocious but yet unchallenged mind enjoying mischievous intellectual pranks, irreverently shocking remarks and speeches, and a "we precious few" rendezvous with the college president's niece, Ellen Rolfe, another individualist, whom he married in 1888. He had already developed an almost automatic reaction against anything given. Present-day undergraduates should know this attitude well. To any proposition, dogma, or assertion, his reaction was to challenge, to analyze ruthlessly, and to dissect clinically. He carried this same deeply ingrained habit, ultimately almost an article of faith, to Johns Hopkins and to

Yale, where he encountered minds that forced him to prove his criticisms. But then came the years of unemployment, with only his father and, after 1888, his wife to challenge him. He finally, thanks to family support and the help of Professor J. L. Laughlin, resumed academic work at Cornell University and then at the University of Chicago, where he moved into the field of political economy, a relatively new field for him. But the hurt of years of neglect and lack of challenge, together with the old habit of almost disdainful intellectual arrogance, carried him into a self-protective and lonely life of his own, shared imperfectly by his sensitive and long-suffering wife. The most puzzling information this writer encountered about Veblen at this stage of his career was his seeming refusal to permit his wife to have a child. The shell, to which Max Lerner refers, was formed by this time, and Veblen wanted no impediments. It would take a skilled analyst to interpret this particular quirk of Veblen's, and one can only record it.

What has been suggested to this point is that Veblen's characteristic methodology, attitude, and peculiar animus were fixed long before he began writing. There is a consistency in his hypercritical approach to anything given. The "placid unbeliever" was a brilliant diagnostician under a veneer of bourgeois tastes. His irregular family and romantic life, which shocked contemporaries at Chicago and Stanford universities, seems to have bothered him relatively little. In R. L. Duffus' *The Innocents at Cedro,* the Duffus boys, who kept house for Veblen after the separation from his first wife, give essentially this same impression.[9] His second marriage, to an idolatrous widow with two daughters who, according to Lubin, tried to "protect him," also seems almost irrelevant.

His family, his wives, and his friends all fitted into the accustomed pattern of people who took care of him but did not
interfere. When anyone really challenged his way of life, as
did David Starr Jordan of Stanford University, his indignation was savage, and the animus showed in his criticisms of
Jordan. His ultimate disillusionment, when there were only
a few devoted disciples (especially Leon Ardzrooni and Wesley Clair Mitchell) and a stepdaughter to care for him, came
as much perhaps from the exhaustion of a way of life as from
professional disappointments. There was a certain determinism in Veblen's way of life from the beginning to the end.

II

Veblen defies labeling. A recent study insists that he was
a socialist.[10] Other labels range all the way from "economic
determinist" to "faker." Today his approach would have the
label "interdisciplinary" and he would be in fashion. The
Carleton Veblen Seminar found him to have been a social
critic of unusually acute perceptions.[11]

Central to Veblen's thought is the concept of the machine
process. Man's command of technology is the measure of
man's evolution. This product of man's instinctive workmanship, if uncontaminated by unproductive motives (such as
profit) or diversionary mythologies (such as organized religions) or power conflicts (such as nationalism), can create an
efficiently operative society. The natural idle curiosity of
man, if allowed full expression, will emancipate man and
permit his true productive powers to operate. To the extent
that any society conforms to the discipline of the machine
process, to that extent is that society efficiently productive

and healthy. To the extent that any society sanctions inhibiting and sabotaging factors, to that extent is that society handicapped.

This technological determinism of Veblen's is rather simplistic as compared with the "technostructure" of John Kenneth Galbraith.[12] However, the elements of the former are to be recognized in the latter. What Veblen could not have foreseen was the degree to which technology, in its manifold forms, would penetrate all of society and enlist virtually everyone in the progressive increase of the gross national product. Even many of those institutionalized forces against which Veblen inveighed have been pushed aside or enlisted.

In Veblen's opinion the primal creative urge, the sense of imagination, and the instinct of workmanship had been stifled over the centuries. They had been perverted by institutions that fed upon the productive forces, utilized mythologies to rationalize control, and diverted the natural powers of man to conspicuous waste and progressive enslavement. A primary cause of this institutionalized exploitation lay in the system of property. The ownership of property by persons or institutions had developed, Veblen suggested, in such a way as to subordinate the welfare of mankind to the objectives and interests of predatory men. This condition persisted during long centuries of primitive technology, but with the coming of modern machine technology a new and revolutionary force entered the lists. At first the old forces either resisted the new technology or tried to control it for their own preservation and strength. However, the ruthless demand of the machine technology for efficiency forced even the most backward and stubborn institutions to change and to adapt themselves. These changes were at times violent, at other times subtle and gradual, but the dynamism of the machine process could not be denied.

Among the most resistive and wasteful of the older institutions was what Veblen called "the pecuniary culture," the business system based on profit. Unfortunately Veblen was not careful in his definition of this culture. He apparently felt that unplanned private enterprise as rationalized by the classical economists, whom he directly attacked as essentially playing games, could not endure indefinitely without explosive revolutionary consequences. Perhaps these would be in the form of bigger depressions, probably in the form of destructive wars, and certainly not in the interests of the multitudes. He studied Karl Marx's analysis and concluded that it was inadequate because it derived from Ricardian and Hegelian concepts no longer viable. He dabbled briefly and rather naively with the idea of having the engineers run society. He was not a reformer, but he was obviously distressed by the failure of modern man to recognize the catastrophic tendencies of the business system. He finally gave up trying to point the way out. He remained a sardonic observer and watched with a macabre sense of humor mankind determined to destroy itself.

The explosive impact of modern technology on primitive societies was patent in his own time and has become a commonplace in ours. The dynamite involved in the rapid take-over of technology in sophisticated societies is only now being fully realized. That this explosiveness has been blunted, resolved, and sublimated by the evolution of a planned economy in the major nations, especially the United States, was something Veblen could not have predicted or foreseen.[13]

One of the more penetrating analyses put forth by Veblen

and later documented by A. A. Berle and Gardiner C. Means, and by subsequent investigations, was the separation of ownership and control.[14] We recognize today that ownership of large-scale corporate enterprises has been distributed, in the form of stock, so that no single individual has a controlling interest unless he is a member of the corporation's board of trustees. And, even for the board, decision-making has become a collective matter. Veblen emphasized the impersonality of the modern corporation, the opportunities for exploitation not only of the laborers but of the stockholders also. What he probably had in mind was the older ideal of owner-manager corporation, long since displaced in large-scale industry.

What he could not have foreseen was the development of collective involvement and responsibility in large-scale industrial enterprises, the gradual obsolescence of the rugged individualist type of entrepreneur, the enormous growth of labor power tempered by increasingly middle class aspirations, and the tremendously increased efficiency of agriculture of corporate character. Instead of the deepening gulf between the "productive" and the "pecuniary" classes, there has been a tremendous growth in gross national product, and a merging of those two elements. Veblen could not predict the development of economic subcultures shoved aside by the macroculture, driven into ghettos, and posing revolutionary threats to the established society. However, Veblen did see the dangers of absentee ownership, and he understood the changing nature of private property ownership in America.

Veblen's businessman was undoubtedly a stereotype of the rugged entrepreneur of the late nineteenth century. It is probably demonstrable that this type survives in America today, but it belongs to the dinosaur age of business. As is demonstrated in Professor Cochran's essay, smaller business has not been swallowed up by the giants but has in fact thrived. Some of it is no doubt of the subcontracting variety, especially in military contracting, but it would be inaccurate to speak of American business as being completely dominated by the large corporations. However, according to Professor Galbraith's analysis, almost all productive enterprise in the United States is interrelated and, even more important, dependent on modern technology. There results a collective commitment, shared even by organized labor, but shared imperfectly. Parts of the population are excluded by reason of race or inadequate education. Galbraith calls this collective situation the "technostructure." [15]

The extent to which the ideology of the business society permeates all of society is illustrated by Veblen in certain areas, especially in his treatment of salesmanship and creation of mythical values. Here he and Galbraith come very close. It is the latter's contention that the market is actually created by the corporate planning through market analysis. Whereas advertising is as old as the hills, salesmanship is a modern development utilizing knowledge of depth psychology and the techniques of opinion research. Veblen also emphasized the role of myth and the prevalence of artificial values. He would be right at home in present-day market analysis. He might be somewhat surprised at the extent of governmental regulation of standards, but he would still find people tending to buy by label rather than by value (although there can be a coincidence of these).

Veblen attacked certain other features of his society. Some of the attacks were valid, others perhaps now only quaint.

His attack on the "captain of erudition," the college president, was undoubtedly motivated in part by his indignation on his separation from Stanford University, but it was also directed at the boards of trustees and presidents of universities and colleges. He felt their conception of these institutions was too often as a corporate entity rather than as an enterprise in liberal education. Situations such as Veblen attacked still survive and can undoubtedly be documented. In the larger universities, however, the function of the president and even the board of trustees has become primarily administrative, and control of education has been taken over by faculty committees and by educational deans. *The Higher Learning in America* is still delightful reading, but the situation it described no longer prevails. Oddly enough, Veblen's central idea, the machine process, tended to obscure his conception of what a college or university should be doing. There is a contradiction of sorts between the training in the machine process and his concept of "idle curiosity," the search for new truth. Veblen did not clear up this problem. There are serious gaps in his consideration of music, the arts, and the humanities. He focused on things "matter of fact," on the elimination of waste, on the efficiency of the machine to purify society.

Other ideas of Veblen's that would have to be changed with later experience are "industrial sabotage," that is, the deliberate withholding of efficiency for the sake of profit; and the idea of conspicuous consumption, today dissipated by the vastly expanded opportunities for possession of consumers' goods formerly available only to the rich. Deliberate sabotage for the sake of profit is still present to some extent, but the substitution of market analysis for mere guesswork in produc-

tion has eliminated the sabotage element in the giant corporations and probably in most other corporations also. Veblen
was undoubtedly correct that a good deal of what is marketable
is for conspicuous consumption based on a credit system, and
motivated by emulation and status building. Ironically, as one
of the seminar students acutely observed, in the wealthier
classes the tendency has been toward conspicuous nonconsump-
tion.

Like any intelligent observer, Veblen was appalled by the
waste of war. And there is still much of value in his criticism
of a society which utilizes patriotism to bolster the market,
whether it does so consciously or not. Since World War II we
have seen the role of armaments and space research increase
in importance. As Professor Friday's essay suggests, Veblen
saw that a choice had to be made between a rational socialized
state and a perpetual war economy. The latter seems to have
become increasingly the choice. Veblen's excoriating and clin-
ical description of patriotism is unhappily too accurate to be
overlooked. Patriotism wedded to modern technology in the
hands of ambitious men or dynasties produces dangers both
obvious and terrifying. Germany under the Hohenzollerns
and later under Hitler is an example, as is Japan under the
feudalistic militarists or, potentially, America under super-
Americans.

Veblen's major contribution was that of one who could lift
himself above the turmoil of his time and take the long view.
Sardonic he might have been, ironic and bitter he became,
but from his evolutionary perspective he saw what few others
of his time were able to discern; that mankind, especially the
American variety, was headed toward unprecedented dangers
requiring greater wisdom than Veblen saw about him. He

would be pleased to see some of his apprehensions about the role of the machine process dissipated. He would have felt justified in his faith that modern technology would, by its very nature, force rationalization and efficiency. He would probably have even been somewhat relieved by the changes in American education. Today he *might* have been safely tucked into a research professorship or the Institute for Advanced Studies; one hopes so. But he would have been appalled by the seemingly untouched subcultures of race and class, and he would have viewed the approach of Armageddon as even closer than in his own time. There will be few to dispute the claim that Veblen was America's greatest social critic of the first half of the twentieth century. It is perhaps too much to ask that the second half of the century produce another such brilliant diagnostician.

Veblen on the Future of American Capitalism

Charles B. Friday

I

THORSTEIN VEBLEN was in his lifetime, and he remains today, a controversial figure among social scientists. That his ideas are still controversial is testimony to their continued vitality and relevance. The reason for contemporary interest in Veblen may well stem from his startling insights into the overriding issues of modern economic society. He was virtually the only American economist of his day concerned with what we now call economic development. Most of his contemporaries confined themselves to the static analysis of the operations of a market economy. To the significant question, Where does all this lead? They remained silent. Some even went so far as to exclude such inquiry from the proper concern of economic theory.

Veblen's hostile criticism of classical and neoclassical economic thought [1] led to his being accused of ruining his students for theoretical work in economics or of being anti-theoretical himself. Yet, as he appropriately pointed out to Davenport, his first two books were called *The Theory of the*

Leisure Class and *The Theory of Business Enterprise.*[2] Veblen's criticism of orthodox economics was not criticism of theory itself, nor was it that orthodox theory was wrong, given its preconceptions and assumptions. It was just that orthodox economic theory was irrelevant to the major problems of modern society. The outcome of its method, at its best, is a body of logically consistent propositions concerning the normal relations of things—a system of economic taxonomy. At its worst, it is a body of maxims for the conduct of business and a polemical discussion of disputed points of policy." [3]

The important questions, to Veblen, concerned the direction of economic change. Economists, as social scientists, he insisted, must produce a theory of economic evolution. To conceive of economic theory as only a static analysis of resource allocation is to avoid scientific responsibility. A theory of economic development should be the very heart of economic science.

It is Veblen's theory, not his lack of it, that makes his work of lasting importance. Even his infamous repetition is understandable (if not always excusable) in that it consists of reminding the reader of his theoretical framework. Veblen attempts to put into meaningful relationship the significant political, social, and economic events that go into shaping evolutionary change. It is theory showing the "grand design" after the manner of a Marx or a Smith rather than a Marshall. It does not isolate the infinitesimal, leaving other things to remain equal. It rather focuses upon the broad sweep of history and the interrelations of institutions and events. The other things that remain equal in neoclassical theory are the very things that are examined by Veblen.

Veblen attacked the central issues. The future of capitalism was his continuing concern, and as a central issue it hardly needs justifying. In this matter he stands in the company of Marx and Schumpeter, the other great theoreticians of the development of capitalism. To Veblen, as to Marx and Schumpeter, capitalism is a transitory system. It will not always be with us. Such a position is controversial, and those who hold it, for whatever reasons, are inclined to be a bit suspect, at least by the orthodox. Those who believe that the Keynesian-type policies of the welfare state have saved capitalism, and that this system can continue indefinitely, are inclined to view heterodox thought today as either simple wrong headedness or, at worst, heresy.

Veblen's reasons for believing capitalism is doomed are different from those of either Marx or Schumpeter, although he is clearly closer to Marx than to Schumpeter. Capitalism, as we have known it, will give way to something else just as feudalism gave way to capitalism. The cause lies in the social irreconcilability of the institutions of private property and the market system with advancing technology. While private property was not especially inappropriate to a society whose level of technological advancement was that of eighteenth century Europe, it is not appropriate to twentieth century industrial societies. Advancing technology is so increasing the capacity to produce goods that private property rights are hampering and retarding the full utilization of resources.

Unlike Marx, Veblen is nonteleological. He is not sure what kind of system will follow capitalism. That depends upon many historical factors. He never ceased to emphasize the "drift of history." The probabilities for the proximate future, however, appeared to him to be either a form of socialism or a militaristic nationalism. It might be noted that Veblen fully predicted a militaristic nationalism for Germany long before the Nazis came to power. However, for the United States, which Veblen took as the prototype of an advanced capitalist economy, he left the two alternatives. The drift of history would determine which.

Also unlike Marx, Veblen issued no call to action. He neither urged one direction over the other, nor did he ever take an active part in politics himself. His concern, he insisted, was not "what ought to be done, but what is to take place." [4] This Olympian attitude has frequently been criticized. Although he is quick to perceive the preconceptions of others, Veblen is nowhere explicit about his own. He proclaims scientific detachment. Yet two values stand out in all Veblen's writing. One is the goal of maximum production. The other is an egalitarianism, or at least a dislike of institutionally imposed or created inequality. Both these values, as we shall see, dominate his analysis.

II

The key to Veblen's theory of capitalism lies in his famous distinction between business and industry, a distinction which Clarence Ayres has generalized into one between institutions and technology.[5] To Veblen, business consists of those institutions associated with making profits in money terms, very largely the institution of private property and its associated "rights." Industry is associated with the technology of making goods, or what he called "the machine process." If the distinction between business and industry is not entirely obvious, it is a consequence of being brought up in a capitalist society whose ideology holds that one makes the most money by making the most useful, efficient, or beautiful goods. The world is supposed to beat a path to the door of the better mousetrap maker and make him wealthy. Business and industry are seen as synonymous activities, and even the words are used interchangeably.

Yet the functions are separate and distinct. In pre-capitalist times the distinction was apparent. Aristotle, in the first book of *Politics,* distinguishes between moral and immoral acquisition. In his view, moral acquisition was directed toward the production of goods to provide for the needs and satisfactions of the population. Immoral acquisition was concerned with acquiring money as an end in itself. Later in history the medieval ethical system, in an attempt to protect society from individual selfishness, banned usury and held to a doctrine of "just price." These doctrines made a clear attempt to control money making as distinct from the production of goods.

Industry (that is, technology or the machine process) is, for Veblen, the strategic, growth-inducing factor in modern civilization. The true meaning of the industrial revolution lies in the advance of human skills and tools. Technology must play some part in all theories of economic development, although different theoreticians assign it different roles. In Veblen's model of economic development, technology plays such a crucial role that he has often been labeled a technological determinist. Although such is not quite the case, as we shall see later, technology does for him have an existence all its own. It is basically exogenous to the business system. One invention calls for another. Technological progress is unceasing and unremitting. It is the dynamic factor in human progress and the key to modern economic history.

The second determinant of capitalist development is the

business system—the institutions that surround the industrial process. These institutions grew up in western Europe in the eighteenth century and replaced much of the medieval pattern of thought and behavior. The system of property rights that is at the heart of the system, and most eloquently articulated by John Locke, is itself a result of technological advance in the eighteenth century. The appearance of a handicraft economy along with the technology of ocean shipping and trade made serious inroads into the medieval institutions of status and prowess and laid the material, historical basis of the right of ownership. In Veblen's words, "The scope to the right of ownership in later modern times is an outgrowth of the exigencies of mercantile traffic, of the prevalence of purchase and sale in a 'money economy.' " [6] Ownership as a right, says Veblen, has as its methaphysical basis man's "assumed creative efficiency as a workman." [7] By Locke's time the ideas that labor is the original source of wealth and hence the basis of ownership could hardly be questioned. And ownership normally meant absolute ownership "with free and unqualified discretion in the use and disposal of the things owned." [8]

The classical economists developed a sophisticated reconciliation between business and industry. Believing society to be best served by the expansion of production (a view which Veblen shared), they argued that the free pursuit of money making by businessmen could accomplish this end (a view which Veblen did not share). An elaborate nexus of competitive behavior would provide the "invisible hand" that would lead businessmen's search for wealth to promote the socially desirable industrial process. An outrageous idea to the medieval mind, it came in time to be the commonplace of men's thinking.

Veblen argued that the system of natural rights favoring

money making was not inappropriate to the eighteenth century economy of small industry and petty trade. It served as an attack on powerful and aristocratic institutions that were holding back economic development. Industrial technology, tied to the business system, produced a huge surge of output; and Veblen appreciated its productive capabilities, although he did not dwell upon them. "So obvious are these good results and so well and widely has the matter been expounded, theoretically, that it is not only permissible, but it is a point of conscience to shorten this tale by passing over these good effects as a matter of common notoriety." [9]

It is the prolonged consequencces of the linking of business and industry that concern Veblen. Though their early compatibility produced the remarkable "good results," the continually changing and advancing industrial technology came to be incompatible with the static business institutions. The universality of petty trade and small industry was, by the early twentieth century, a thing of the past. The changing technology had produced giant firms and world-wide markets. That "simple and obvious system of natural liberty" ceased to be relevant to the modern world. As Veblen points out: "Natural rights, as they found their way into law and equity, were in effect the assumed equal rights of men so situated on a plane of at least constructive equality that the individuals concerned would be left in a position of effectively free choice if conventional restrictions were done away." [10] The development of technologically efficient giant firms had eliminated men from that "plane of at least constructive equality" that was the social foundation of property rights. Capitalism had produced immense inequalities among men. In Veblen's view, its business elite came to be as restrictive of further economic development as the landed aristocracy had been in the earlier period.

It is the restrictive effects of business domination of the industrial process in the modern world that pervade all Veblen's writing. In this connection he may be likened to Adam Smith, whose prime concern was the restrictive consequences of mercantilist domination of industry in an earlier day. Both held maximum production to be socially desirable. Both saw, in their respective eras, the institutions controlling production to be engaged in restrictive practices. That they attacked different institutions is simply because they lived in different times with control in different hands.

A description of this aspect of modern capitalism is best presented in Veblen's own words:

Industry is carried on for the sake of business, and not conversely: the process and activity of industry are conditioned by the outlook of the market, which means the presumptive chance of business profits. . . . The economic welfare of the community at large is best served by a facile and uninterrupted interplay of the various forces which make up the industrial system at large; but the pecuniary interests of the business men in whose hands lies the discretion in the matter are not necessarily best served by an unbroken maintenance of the industrial balance.[11]

Moreover, the system of property rights gives wide freedom to the businessman. "Business management has a chance to proceed on a temperate and sagacious calculation of profit and loss, untroubled by sentimental considerations of human kindness or irritation or of honesty." [12] This freedom might have done little social harm in a fairly egalitarian and highly competitive economy, but the invisible hand, presumed to protect society's interest, was no longer effective.

In the first place, the growth of monopoly allowed the

businessman to improve his well-being at the expense of the community. The disclosures in Veblen's day of the activities of the railroads and the Standard Oil Company, of the trusts and holding companies, of stock watering and financial scandals testified to the antisocial behavior of large-scale, monopolistic business enterprise. But it was not only the spectacular disclosures of greed that provided evidence of the incompatibility of business and industry; normal, day-to-day, accepted business activities were in constant conflict with industrial growth. It had become a commonplace of economic practice that large-scale enterprise, with some degree of control over supply, might make more money by restricting output than by expanding it. The existence of excess capacity in ordinary (at least nonwar) times was an increasingly common observable phenomenon. Furthermore the restrictive practices of monopoly were calling forth similar attempts on the part of laborers, physicians, farmers, small businessmen, and others who could, through organization or association, restrict the supply of their goods or services in an attempt to make more money for themselves. The final outcome of such widespread restriction could hardly be socially desirable.

Moreover, the element of monopoly restriction is not confined to single firm monopolies. Veblen recognized at least thirty years before Chamberlin the restrictive phenomenon of monopolistic competition.[13] Writing in 1904, Veblen says:

But it is very doubtful if there are any successful business ventures within the range of modern industries from which the monopoly element is wholly absent. There are, at any rate, few and not of great magnitude. And the endeavor of all such enterprises that look to a permanent continuance of their business is to establish as much of a monopoly as may be. Such a monopoly position may be a legally established one, or one due to location or the control of natural resources, or it may be a monopoly of a less definite character resting on custom and prestige (good will). This latter class of monopolies are not commonly classed as such; although in character and degree the advantage which they give is very much the same as that due to a differential advantage in location or in the command of resources. The end sought by the systematic advertising of the larger business concerns is such a monopoly of custom and prestige. This form of monopoly is sometimes of great value, and is frequently sold under the name of good-will, trade marks, brands, etc. . . . .

The great end of consistent advertising is to establish such differential monopolies resting on popular conviction.[14]

It is to be noted that Veblen did not see competition ending with the advent of such monopolistic devices. It simply becomes inter-industry rather than intra-industry as in the classical model. "The result is not that competition ceases or declines . . . but only that it takes a new turn, commonly with an increased vigor and persistence. . . . It becomes a competition not within the business, but between this business as a whole and the rest of the community." [15] This kind of competition places increased emphasis on "vendibility" of commodites rather than "serviceability."

The vital point of production with [the businessman] is the vendibility of the output, its convertibility into money values, not its serviceability for the needs of mankind. A modicum of serviceability, for some purpose or other, the output must have if it is to be salable. But it does not follow that the highest serviceability gives the largest gains to the business man in terms of money, nor does it follow that the output need in all cases have other than factitious serviceability.[16]

This aspect of modern capitalism has been so widely commented upon in recent years that it needs no elaboration

here. It is, for Veblen, simply a further unhealthy manifesta-
tion of business domination of industry.

In the second place, the recurrence of recessions and depressions interferes with the industrial process. The dominance of the business ideology is so great that sometimes we
forget that recessions are the result of businessmen's collective
decisions that they can make more money (or lose less) by
closing down their operations than by continuing production.
Veblen points out, "The notion is never seriously enter-
tained that there is or might be an embarrassing excess of
goods, or the appliances for their production, above what
would be of some human use if the business situation permitted them to be turned to that use." [17]

Veblen is generally characterized as having an inadequate
theory of crises or depressions. He lacked a theory of aggregate demand that epitomized the work of Keynes. However,
his analysis of the role of financial institutions in capital
formation is much like that of Keynes, and his theory in general is consistent with rather than contradictory of Keynes. [18]

On the basis of his analysis, Veblen held the view that
"chronic depression, more or less pronounced, is normal to
business under the fully developed regime of the machine
industry." [19] His theory is basically one of stagnation (that
is, chronic depression) rather than crisis. Lapses from stagnation come from exogenous forces such as war. In *Absentee
Ownership,* he concludes that normally:

Free-swung production, approaching the full productive capacity of
the equipment and available manpower, was no longer to be toler-
ated in ordinary times. It became even more imperative to observe
a duly graduated moderation, and to govern the volume of output,
not by the productive capacity of the plant or the working capacity

of the workmen, nor by the consumptive needs of the consumers, but by what the traffic would bear; which was then habitually and increasingly coming to mean a modicum of unemployment both of plant and the available manpower.[20]

Although Veblen fails to tie monopoly and depression together in rigorous fashion, he sees them supplementing each other. Monopolistic practices are, in part, an outgrowth of the tendency toward depression. The "expedient of coalition" is one of the tools of the businessman to restrict output in order to keep prices from falling. In so doing, unemployment is aggravated and the depression intensified and prolonged.

The third area of conflict between business and industry lies in the tendency of the business system toward wasteful production.

The normal result of business control of industry—normal in the sense of being uniformly aimed at and also in that it commonly follows—is the accumulation of wealth and income in the hands of a class. Under the well-accepted principle of "conspicuous waste" wealth so accumulated is to be put in evidence in visible consumption and visible exemption from work. So that with due, but ordinarily not a large, lapse of time, an elaborate scheme of proprieties establishes itself, bearing on the matter of conspicuous consumption, so contrived as to "take up the slack." [21]

The "elaborate scheme of proprieties" is, of course, detailed in *The Theory of the Leisure Class.*

The consequence of this waste is to inhibit economic growth. For Veblen, growth is dependent not only upon technology but also upon the use to which that part of the output in excess of essential consumption and replacement cost of machinery is put. He calls this surplus the "net product." [22] With increasing technological efficiency, the size of the "net product" may be considerable: "But owing to the very high productive efficiency of modern mechanical industry, the margin available for wasteful occupations and wasteful expenditures is very great. The requirements of the aggregate livelihood are so far short of the possible output of goods by modern methods as to leave a very wide margin for waste and parasitic income." [23]

The use to which the "net product" is put is a matter of human institution. In this sense Veblen is again akin to Adam Smith. Smith held that other than monopoly, unproductive labor was the chief deterrent to economic growth. Veblen's conspicuous waste appears to be basically the same as Smith's unproductive labor. Veblen argues that too much of the "net product" is used for conspicuous waste rather than for productive purposes just as Smith argued that labor should be channeled into productive capital formation rather than used as servants for the rich and the like.

It should be noted that this long-neglected idea has crept back into the analysis of development theories when applied to backward nations. The use of vast wealth for land owning, precious jewel collections, building of temples, and conspicuous consumption of feudal princes rather than for capital formation is deplored as inhibiting economic growth. It is easy to observe such phenomena in India or Saudi-Arabia. The same analysis is rarely applied to advanced nations such as the United States.

Veblen, however, pointed out that the institutions of modern capitalism, through its leisure class, may direct resources to conspicuous waste precisely as feudal institutions do. It is the great inequalities produced by capitalism that account for this waste. Veblen returns again and again to the industrially inhibiting effects of inequality.

Veblen thus sees society's goal of maximum production of useful and efficient goods hampered by the businessman's concern with maximizing profits. The consequence is monopolistic restrictions of output, excess capacity of firms, chronic unemployment, and conspicuous waste. Before we see the outcome of this process we must turn to his theory of politics.

III

Unlike the orthodox economists of his day, Veblen saw no separation between economics and politics. All his work on American capitalism contains much political theory as well as an integration of economics and politics. It is the unity of economics and politics in Veblen's theory of capitalism that has been important in generating both praise for him as a social scientist and criticism for his lack of orthodoxy.

In tracing its evolution, Veblen finds that government "was once an organization for the control of affairs in the interest of princely or dynastic ends." However, in modern times "business ends have taken the lead of dynastic ends in statecraft." [24] In more detail, he says:

Because of this settled habit of seeing all the conjunctures of life from the business point of view, in terms of profit and loss, the management of affairs of the community at large falls by common consent into the hands of business men and is guided by business considerations. Hence modern politics is business politics, even apart from the sinister application of the phrase, to what is invidiously called corrupt politics. This is true of both foreign and domestic policy. Legislation, police surveillance, the administration of justice, the military and diplomatic services are all chiefly concerned with business relations, pecuniary interests, and they have little more than incidental bearing on other human interests.[25]

It is easy to recognize some similarity between this statement and the Marxian theory of the state, as it is when Veblen says, "representative government means, chiefly, represen-
tation of business interests." [26] However, Veblen finds a
nexus between his notion of the state and modern democracy
with constitutional rules that is not apparent in Marx. Although constitutions are primarily involved with private property rights and securing the continuation of the institutional
structure, democracy in Veblen's view has made no serious
inroads upon this purpose. The reason democracy has not
disrupted the institutional structure is that the "underlying
population" has been conditioned to want business control of
the state. The primary means of such conditioning is through
the ancient and powerful appeal of patriotism. The successful
linking of patriotism and property in the modern world as-
sures business domination of the state.

By force of this happy knack of clannish fancy [between patriotism
and property] the common man is enabled to feel that he has some
sort of metaphysical share in the gains which accrue to the business
men who are citizens of the same "commonwealth"; so that whatever policy furthers the commercial gains of those business men
whose domicile is within the national boundaries is felt to be bene-
ficial to all the rest of the population.[27]

Unlike Marx, Veblen sees no inevitable clash between the
proletariat and the capitalist. Such a clash may arise, but it is
in no sense inevitable. In fact, much of Veblen's analysis is
an attempt to show that patriotism and national integrity—
deeply rooted habits of thinking that once served the purpose
of group survival—are so ingrained in people's thought that
no such confrontation may take place. That these ways of
thinking may be obsolete in modern technologically advanced

societies does not diminish their force. In this way, Veblen explains why, even in times of crisis, class solidarity does not appear. His theory in this respect is much superior to Marx's, or at least to that of the less sophisticated Marxists.

IV

We are now in a position to pull together the strands of Veblenian thought in order to get a glimpse of the future. The consequences of business domination of industry and politics in the modern period are economic stagnation—a failure to maintain adequate rates of economic growth—and the use of considerable quantities of resources for conspicuous waste, not only by the leisure class but also by those who would emulate them. The business institution of property, appropriate to the eighteenth century when it emerged as an attack on feudal institutions, has ceased to be appropriate to technologically advanced societies. Just as the technology of the industrial revolution broke the bonds of feudalism, so the advancing technology of the twentieth century will destroy the institutions of capitalism.

Broadly, the machine discipline acts to disintegrate the institutional heritage, of all degrees of antiquity and authenticity—whether it be the institutions that embody the principle of natural liberty or those that comprise the residue of more archaic principles of conduct still current in civilized life. It thereby cuts away that ground of law and order on which business enterprise is founded.[28]

And again, "[private property] cannot, in the long run, get along with the machine process." [29]

What, then, is to follow in the wake of capitalism? The other great theoreticians of the demise of capitalism, Marx

and Schumpeter, thought socialism would follow. Veblen is
less sure. It is true that for Veblen the logic of the machine
process should lead to the removal of the control of industry
from those who would only make money from it and put it in
the hands of those who would use it for maximum social
benefit. In 1904, in *The Theory of Business Enterprise,* Veblen appears to consider some such socialism to be a strong
possibility. As industrialization progresses, he then argued,
more and more of the underlying population will be subject
to the discipline of the machine process. Veblen believed that
this would result in a standarization of the workman's intellectual life in terms of mechanical processes and would make
him suspicious of ceremonial, institutional thinking.

What the discipline of the machine industry inculcates, therefore,
in the habits of life and of thought of the workman, is regularity of
sequence and mechanical precision; and the intellectual outcome is
an habitual resort to terms of measurable cause and effect, together
with a relative neglect and disparagement of such exercise of the
intellectual faculties as does not run on these lines.[30]

Furthermore, industrialization, through urbanization and
increasing the numbers of people who gain their income by
selling their labor services, lessens the desire to acquire property compared to a rural, frontier, farming society. In its
place he thought he saw the development of a trade union
spirit that cut seriously into the old notion of property rights.
"The principle that man may do what he will with his own is
losing its binding force with large classes in the community,
apparently because the spiritual ground on which rests the
notion of "his own" is being cut away by the latter day experience of these classes." [31]

Thus, in 1904, Veblen believed that inroads were being
made into the old notions of property by industrialization. It

was an occupational theory rather than a class theory. Veblen believed that socialism was finding adherents among the skilled mechanical trades and those engaged in mechanical agriculture. However, he recognized that there is nothing in the machine process *per se* that inculcates socialistic notions. It may do so for some occupations, but it also creates white collar and managerial occupations that are trained to pecuniary pursuits. These occupations are immune to socialism. Thus industrialization segregates wage earners into two categories, making class solidarity unlikely if not impossible.

Another deterrent to the spread and acceptance of socialistic ideas arises from leisure class leadership. The conservatism of the leisure class imparts a general conservatism to the community at large. In order to maintain self-respect each stratum of society must emulate its betters by dressing in the latest styles, following the sporting events, keeping up their automobiles, TV sets, or whatever status symbol is current. Maintaining the requirements of "pecuniary decency" leaves little income, time, or energy for revolutionary activities.

These counter forces opposing socialism appear to Veblen, at least by the 1920s, to be as strong, if not stronger, than the technological forces that might lead to socialism. Indeed, Veblen is critical of Marx for his faith in the proletariat pursuing its own economic self-interest. The conditioning of capitalism appears to Veblen to be too much to be overcome in the immediate future.

Veblen followed the Russian Revolution with interest and sympathy. In a series of articles in *The Dial* he argued that "circumstantial evidence, backed by official reports" appears on the whole to indicate that Russian socialism is a viable system working with passable efficiency.[32]

The most significant reason socialism has gained little hold

in the United States, however, is associated with war and
patriotism. And this, in turn, provides the alternative system
which, for Veblen, may well follow capitalism. Veblen refers
to it as a militaristic-nationalism arising from an alignment
of business and military classes. This alternative follows logically from Veblen's theory of politics.

The manner in which business interests work out in government
policy may be shown by following up their bearing upon one phase
of this policy. An extreme expression of business politics, and at the
same time a characteristic trait of higher levels of national life in
Christendom, is the current policy of war and armaments.[33]

The policy of war and armaments serves the requisites of
technologically advanced capitalism. It provides the necessary
waste to take up the slack of productive facilities over and
above consumption and replacement of machinery (Veblen's
net product) which is not already taken up by conspicuous
consumption. Because of the increasing productivity of the
machine process, the margin available for such waste is increasing. In addition, the patriotic nature of warlike policy
"makes for a conservative animus on the part of the population" [34] and counteracts any socialistic tendencies that may
arise from the logic of the machine process or be transmitted
from socialistic countries abroad.

Lest it be misunderstood, it should be pointed out that
Veblen is not holding to a "plot theory of history" or a "devil
theory of history." War and arms races are not deliberately
conceived of by governments as a means of combatting subversive movements at home or of producing wasteful goods. It
is simply that historical events have generated conditions
which make these actions the consequence of the business
system.

The modern warlike policies are entered upon for the sake of peace, with a view to the orderly pursuit of business. In their initial motive they differ from the warlike dynastic policies of the sixteenth, seventeenth, and eighteenth centuries. But the disciplinary effects of the warlike pursuits and of warlike preoccupations are much the same whatever may be their initial motive or ulterior aim. The end sought in the one case was warlike mastery and high repute in the matter of ceremonial precedence; in the other, the modern case, it is pecuniary mastery and high repute in the matter of commercial solvency. But in both cases alike the pomp and circumstance of war and armaments, and the sensational appeals to patriotic pride and animosity made by victories, defeats, or comparisons of military and naval strength, act to rehabilitate lost ideals and weakened convictions of the chauvinistic or dynastic order. At the same stroke they direct the popular interest to other, nobler, institutionally less hazardous matters than the unequal distribution of wealth or creature comforts.[35]

The course of an armaments race not only becomes a corrective for social unrest, but it also opens the door for an attack upon capitalism from another direction.

[Experience] argues that when warlike emulation between states of somewhat comparable force has once got underway it assumes a cumulative character; so that a scale of expenditure for armaments which would at the outset have seemed absurdly impossible comes presently to be accepted as a matter of course. . . . In this cumulative diversion of effort to warlike ends a point is presently reached beyond which the question of armament is no longer, What amount of warlike expenditure is needed to extend or maintain business traffic? but rather What amount will the nation's resources bear?[36]

The consequences for business enterprise of prolonged military build-up may be disastrous. The ends of national policy may shift from "business advantage to dynastic ascendency." The military may gain sufficient power "as to sacrifice the profits of the businessman to the exigencies of the higher politics." [37] Business may become no more than the fiscal ways and means for achieving the higher ideals of national power and glory.

Veblen asks, why should not business call a halt to the armaments race when armaments become an end in themselves? If governments serve business interests, how can they turn against business? His answer is twofold. First: "So long as the pecuniary inducements held out by the state, in bidding for funds or supplies overbalance the inducements offered by alternative lines of employment, the businessmen will supply these demands, regardless of what the ulterior substantial outcome of such a course may be in the end." [38] And, second, vast fortunes are made in the process of supplying military needs. An alliance may be possible in which business profits are secured and power goes to the military. The underlying population may live at moderately decent levels with the servile status appropriate to a garrison state.

Should this be the case, capitalism as it was known in its heyday will be as dead as if it were overthrown by a Marxian revolution. The rights of property, as well as other "natural rights," would become subservient to the will of the dynastic state.

Thus Veblen sees, in any event, the demise of capitalism. The one road to its death may be socialism. The alternative is a nationalistic militarism which will be equally fatal.

Natural rights being a by-product of peaceful industry, they cannot be reinstated by a recourse to warlike habits and a coercive government, since warlike habits and coercion are alien to the natural-rights spirit. Nor can they be reinstated to a recourse to settled peace and freedom, since an era of settled peace and freedom would push on the dominance of the machine process and the large business, which break down the system of natural liberty. [39]

He concludes: "It seems possible to say this much, that the full dominion of business enterprise is necessarily a transitory dominion. It stands to lose in the end whether the one or the other of the two divergent cultural tendencies wins, because it is incompatible with the ascendency of either." [40]

V

Since Veblen's day a third alternative—neither socialist nor fascist—has been proposed: Welfare Capitalism. Its leading theoretician was John Maynard Keynes, and its most articulate and convincing exponent is John Kenneth Galbraith. In the United States this new "middle way" began to take shape in the 1930s with the New Deal, when American capitalism faced its most severe crisis. In the midst of the great depression it appeared that one or the other of Veblen's alternatives was approaching. Veblen's writings gained an audience that they had never been able to reach in his lifetime. Yet Keynes's policies, aimed at saving capitalism, attracted the attention of many intellectuals and some policy makers. They seemed to offer a safe and sane way out of the crisis without doing violence to the basic institutions of capitalism. At the base was the simple proposal to use the traditional powers of the capitalist state to channel the money-making desires of the private sector into industrially useful purposes. The chief means of accomplishing this was to be through taxing, spending, and control of the money supply, although some additional social legislation might be required.

The nature of the government activity, in almost all cases, turned out to require an egalitarian bent, as Keynes took pains to point out.[41] Its egalitarianism, within the basic institutional structure of capitalism, appealed to all liberals and even to some radicals. Although conservative opposition was forceful for many years, by the 1960s Welfare Capitalism had become the orthodoxy of both professional economists and most government policy makers.[42]

Veblen has been criticized for failing to take into account the possibility that social legislation and control of business by government might greatly meliorate the defects of capitalism and thus, by improving its performance, perpetuate it indefinitely.[43] His failure to do so, according to Professor Hill, stems from what is believed to be an inadequate and one-sided theory of the state.

If Veblen failed in this respect, his theory of the state is but partially responsible. His basic concept of the conflict between business and industry leads inevitably to the conclusion that no institutional structure can continue indefinitely. The inexorable march of technology renders all former institutions obsolete in time. Unless technological advance comes to a halt, an unlikely prospect, capitalism, even Welfare Capitalism, cannot continue indefinitely. It is his basic theoretical framework of the functioning of the economy, not just his theory of the state, that leads to this conclusion.

It could be argued that his nonteleological approach and his continual emphasis on the drift of history do not preclude Welfare Statism as a temporary stopgap to the problems with which he was concerned. Such may be the case. However, I am inclined to think that Veblen would not have viewed the Welfare State as it exists in the United States as saving American capitalism, at least for very long.

Veblen nowhere directs his undivided attention to a possible Welfare State solution to the problems of capitalism.

However, some clue to his thought in these matters is available. He was definitely hostile to social democratic movements in Europe which proposed basically what is today the Welfare State. He believed them to be largely ineffective. "In practical politics the Social Democrats have had to make up their account with the labor movement, the agricultural population, and the imperialist policy." [44] By embracing business unionism, peasant ownership, and chauvinistic jingoism, they have accepted the basic institutions of the business system and with it the domination of business principles in politics as well as economics. Had he lived to see it, Veblen might have noted that Britain's Labour Government was willing to increase domestic unemployment in order to stabilize the value of the pound for international business transactions.

He was equally scornful of reformers:

Not that it is hereby intended to cast a slur on these meritorious endeavors to save mankind by treating symptoms. The symptoms treated are no doubt evil, as they are said to be. . . . The endeavors in question are beside the point in that they do not fall into the shape of a business proposition. They are, on the whole, not so profitable a line of investment as certain other ventures that are open to modern enterprise. Hence, if they traverse the course of business and of industrial exigencies, they are nugatory, being in the same class with the labor of Sisyphus; whereas if they coincide in effect with the line along which business and industrial exigencies move, they are a work of supererogation, except so far as they may be conceived to accelerate a change that is already underway.[45]

Veblen regards the egalitarian reformers as treating symptoms and not basic causes. The basic causes, there can be no doubt, lie in the natural rights institutions, particularly private property. Elsewhere he notes that liberals "are ready to disallow the vested rights of privilege but will not consent to disallow the vested rights of ownership." [46] And it is the "vested rights of ownership" that are in most serious conflict with the advance of technology.

Veblen's theory of the state, of course, supplements his economic argument. He notes: "It seldom happens, if at all, that the government of a civilized nation will persist in a course of action detrimental or not ostensibly subservient to the interests of the more conspicuous body of the community's business men." [47] It might be argued that the Welfare State is not in conflict even with Veblen's theory of the state. Welfare reforms may have interfered little, if at all, with the "vested rights of ownership" and may be in no way detrimental "to the more conspicuous body of the community's business men." Welfare Capitalism may have made the "right to profit" more secure than ever before.

Perhaps a better approach is to ask to what extent the Welfare State has produced the required institutional changes to meliorate or eliminate the Veblenian problems. The problems are, as we noted before, monopolistic restrictions, excess capacity, a tendency toward recession in the absence of exogenous forces, and the use of sizable amounts of resources for waste and conspicuous consumption rather than for growth and human welfare.

The Welfare State does not seem to have solved the latter problem, at least in the minds of many contemporary observers. Veblen first levied this criticism of capitalism in *The Theory of the Leisure Class* in 1899. Nearly sixty years later Professor Galbraith, in his best-selling book, *The Affluent Society*,[48] made essentially the same charge. Modern capitalism produces wasteful goods of little urgent need while urgently needed goods go unproduced or produced in insufficient quantity. Galbraith argued that, to date, Welfare Capitalism has failed to secure an adequate social balance between the output of the private sector and the output of the public sector of goods and services for human consumption. We thus produce an abundance of private goods from elaborate motor cars to electric swizzle sticks rather than needed hospitals and sewage-disposal plants. This is precisely the point Veblen was making. Conspicuous consumption means foregoing the production of goods that are more urgently needed. Veblen argued that once a subsistence is achieved, surplus productive capacity is used to produce goods designed to raise one's standing in the community rather than to enrich one's life. Public goods cannot, by their nature, raise the relative status of individuals except in a perverse way (for example, a paved country road leading to the governor's property).

On the surface, at least, there appears to be a great deal of similarity between Galbraith and Veblen. Both men are inveterate phrase makers, both are satirists, both are critical of classical economics (for many of the same reasons), and both are concerned with the problem of "conspicuous waste" or "social imbalance." Yet here the similarity ends. I am afraid Veblen would have put Galbraith in the class of moralists who try to save mankind by treating symptoms rather than basic causes. The source of conspicuous waste, which Galbraith does not treat in any systematic fashion, is Veblen's chief concern. He finds the source in the great inequalities of modern capitalism—inequalities that are partly inherited from earlier societies and are partly created by the business culture. Because modern society is less sharply class stratified than that of older Europe, "the norm of reputability imposed by the upper class extends its coercive influence with but slight hindrance down through the social structure to the lowest strata".[49] The existence of the wealthy causes the poor to waste their money in order to maintain their self-respect. Emulation is a powerful economic motive as both Veblen and Madison Avenue understand. As long as the great inequalities persist, waste will persist,[50] and society cannot expect to use its productive efforts more effectively.

Thus, where Galbraith urges liberals to give up their concern with equality and devote themselves to rectifying the social balance through increasing taxes and public services, Veblen finds that without significant change toward more equality, conspicuous waste is inevitable. No amount of pleading will be successful in eliminating it.

As we have noted before, the great inequalities of capitalism are, in Veblen's view, responsible for many of its ills. Whatever the merits of the statistical debate about whether inequality has decreased or not under the Welfare State, it is apparent that great economic inequality continues to exist. Professor Ayres has pointed out that "the industrial revolution has brought into existence a way of life which, for the first time in human experience, makes inequality unnecessary." [51] Although it may be unnecessary, the institutional structure has not yet cracked sufficiently to render it unreal.

One of the more striking pieces of evidence that the Veblenian problem has not been eliminated is the increasing concern expressed over "the threat of automation." The "threat" is, of course, to the old institutions. This is not the place for an extended discussion of the problem. The Report of the President's Commission on Automation, Technology, and Economic Growth both presents the problem and indicates the concern of officialdom about the matter. It is sufficient to point out that many are beginning to see the problem in precisely Veblenian terms. We are told we may have to "rethink" the relationship between work and income because we are becoming so productive that it may no longer be necessary for most people to work. "Rethinking" seems inevitably to involve rethinking the whole natural rights question, particularly property rights. That this problem can be solved within the bounds of Welfare Capitalism has yet to be demonstrated.

Other evidence of the Veblenian problem abounds. Spectacular technological success in agriculture produced the seemingly insoluble, and misnamed, "agricultural problem." Congressional hearings revealing antisocial behavior in pharmaceutical and automobile industries are followed by "business as usual." Advertising consumes a portion of the national effort that might surprise even Veblen. He did not live to see the communication miracle of television turned into a gigantic billboard for underarm deodorant. The transportation problem of urban centers is solved by urban renewal, which brings the middle class into the city and moves the slums outside.

The existence of excess capacity and a tendency toward chronic recession, in the absence of external forces, apparently remain problems. During the period between the Korean War and the Vietnam War, this was the major concern of economists and policy makers. That the United States was unable to reach even the minimal goal of 4 per cent unemployed during that period was of constant bother. A good deal of the effort of the President's Council of Economic

Advisers was directed toward measuring the amount of excess capacity in the economy (that is, the gap between actual and potential output) .

Certainly the central economic question of our day is whether or not Welfare Capitalism is a viable alternative to some kind of socialism or a militaristic nationalism, a return to *laissez faire* capitalism being clearly unrealistic. Keynesian theory holds it as a possibility; Veblenian theory appears not to. It is too early to say which is right. In sheer truth, Welfare Capitalism has not yet been tried in the United States. Although some moderate welfare reforms were enacted in the 1930s and a moderate extension made in the 1960s, the burden of "government intervention" has been military, not welfare.

As everybody knows, the social unrest of the Great Depression ended only after the United States entered World War II. The gigantic wartime expenditures brought full employment and united a dissident population. The feared postwar depression did not materialize until 1949 because of a variety of backlog conditions. And from that short-lived depression the United States was saved by the Korean War. From the end of the Korean War until the escalation of the war in Vietnam, stagnation was feared. With the Vietnam War employment rose and prosperity returned.

We know that the Keynesian formal model works. That is, aggregate demand can be sustained by government purchases of military goods. But that point was made in Germany in the 1930s. Whether we will permit government to sustain demand by buying peacetime goods—houses, medical care, pollution control, transporation, and the like—is as yet unknown. We have not tried on a scale adequate to prove the point. To date our most dramatic experiment has been a tax reduction aimed at stimulating demand in the private sector.

What is of serious concern is the tendency of our society toward increasingly warlike activities. Veblen was well aware of this tendency, which, in 1904, he believed to be one aspect of the system. By the 1920s Veblen was convinced that the drift of circumstances was emphasizing this aspect to the exclusion of more peaceful tendencies. The central element in the drift of circumstances was the appearance of Bolshevism or Communism in Russia.

Veblen recognized the Cold War at its inception. In a series of articles in *The Dial* and *The Freeman* he pointed to the irreconcilability of the two systems and the probable reactions of the Western countries. "The civilized nations have come to face a fateful choice between Bolshevism and war." [52] Veblen argued that the appearance of Communism in Russia offered a threat to the vested interests of the "civilized nations" and that they would react with all the means at their disposal to prevent Communism from spreading.

The array of force that the United States has built up to oppose Communism, particularly since World War II, seems to indicate that the drift of circumstances has not much altered the course of "the civilized nations." An obsessive concern with containing Communism with bombs and force, rather than coping with domestic problems or giving aid and support to the aspirations of the peoples of the undeveloped part of the world, may be bringing about that coalition of business and military leaders that Veblen feared. There is considerable evidence of it. Senator Eugene McCarthy in an article in the *Saturday Review* quotes a Defense Department pamphlet, "Information and Guidance on Military Assis-

tance," indicating the close ties of business and military in
selling weapons:

The Department of Defense has embarked on an intensified military assistance sales program. . . .

Achievement of . . . objectives calls for a very substantial increase
over past sales levels. Success in this endeavor will be dependent in
large measure upon effective sales promotion. The DOD has taken
several steps to assist in the successful conclusion of military sales.
. . . Foreign customer preference for U.S. material is being generated by developing an appreciation of its technical superiority,
price, availability, and the offer of follow-on support through U.S.
logistics systems.

In many cases, credit arrangements may be made to facilitate military sales, on short or long term basis as needed.[53]

The final evidence is not yet in. It seems increasingly clear
that the immediate alternatives before American capitalism
are either a Welfare State or a Militaristic Nationalism. No
other forces appear in the offing. Which system has the
greater perseverence is yet to be seen.

Perhaps Veblen was wrong in attributing little strength to
welfare reform movements. His analysis may be too simple,
and sometimes even crude. But he devoted more attention to
the warlike activities of modern society than to its welfare
activities. In that emphasis he appears, so far, to have been
more right than wrong.

Business in Veblen's America

Thomas C. Cochran

ALTHOUGH NEVER A FAVORITE in schools of business, Thorstein Veblen was in fact a pioneer exponent of the study of both business administration and business history. "In so far as the theorist aims to explore the specifically modern economic phenomena," he wrote, "his line of approach must be from the businessman's standpoint, since it is from that standpoint that the course of these phenomena is directed." [1] Seeing the changes in technology and economic organization that were taking place more clearly than most contemporary economists, historians or sociologists, he urged his students to examine real business operations in a broad social context.

Veblen attached great importance to the cumulative growth of the "technological" habits of thought necessary for controlling the machine process. These habits of thought and their related actions comprised a social institution that Veblen called the "industrial arts," one that was often frustrated or opposed by the profit-oriented institutions of business.

Veblen's major ideas appear to have been formed in the late 1880s and early 1890s, a troubled period in American capitalism. From the relationships of workers, entrepreneurs, and the suppliers of services, he developed some principles of capitalist dynamics that proved essentially correct, but others that did not stand the test of time.

In the late nineteenth century America was operating on a low-wage and high-profit basis with the profits invested in rapid industrial expansion. As a few business firms became large and stable enough for public financing, investment bankers took an increasingly prominent part in the allocation of capital. Veblen's fear that big business and big finance would take control of the economy and impose some form of business feudalism mirrored much contemporary thought. For example, in 1899, the year of the publication of *The Theory of the Leisure Class,* the Chicago Civic Association held a great national meeting of businessmen, politicians and academicians to consider the trust problem. Until World War I diverted public interest, fear of the machinations of big business and the financial control of the money trust were perennial matters of national concern.

Subsequent developments show the early twentieth century to have been the peak of influence for investment bankers and the monopoly power of big business, not the beginning of an upward trend. Free enterprise capitalism was not ended, as Veblen expected, by chronic depression and the destructive competition of firms reorganized in bankruptcy. But to say that Veblen was partly misled by the thinking of his time should not obscure the fact that his detached, anthropological approach to the world of business gave new insights.

Certainly business is a pecuniary institution. The small number of big business managers, whom Veblen put outside the ranks of businessmen, may see themselves as professionals, but the two or more million small enterprisers of his time, or the ten million of our own time, are in business to make money. It is also true that in marketing operations, whether in commodities or finance, money can be made from declines in value as well as from increases. In the poorly regulated national markets of the 1890s the operations of speculators were at times a menace to economic progress.

Seeing all the ways in which business could restrict production, raise prices, and upset the economy by speculative activity, Veblen thought there must be a better, more rational way of organizing production and distribution. His solution, which he never clearly defined, was a system run by engineers and other specialists in production for the welfare of society. He shared with many socialists the belief that, rid of the incubus of large-scale capitalism, industrial society would function for the benefit of the ordinary citizen. The experiences of the twentieth century have cast a doubt on this hope. While capitalism has come to function somewhat better, other systems have been shown to have their own endemic weaknesses. The social idealism of the turn of the century has gradually turned to skepticism and, perhaps too great, resignation.

Let us now examine the business scene in which Veblen formed his ideas, and the business history that gave support to his conclusions. Nation-wide competition and large scale operation were as new to the generation growing up after 1850 as atomic power and outer space are to its descendants one hundred years later. The pressures that a national market would impose on production and selling and the opportunities such a market could open to the shrewd and fortunate were all new and all uncertain. Businessmen were also becoming more familiar with the uses and abuses of the corporation, many of which were still mysteries to the ordinary legislator or political leader.

As technology improved and lower railroad rates intensified competition, the rapid adjustments required to maintain a share of any given market were made more difficult by generally falling prices. Between 1873 and the end of 1878, and again from 1893 to 1897, the nation suffered from continuous depression and manufacturers from great overcapacity. When markets had been local or regional it had often been possible to control prices by tacit agreements or by accepting the leadership of one firm. The procedures later became known as monopolistic competition and were what Veblen, no doubt, had in mind when he wrote: "It is very doubtful if there are any successful business ventures within the range of modern industries from which the monopoly element is wholly absent." [2]

In the 1890s new and more systemic efforts were made to maintain prices by agreement. The history of voluntary associations went back to the merchant guilds and the Hanse. In earlier America they had generally been confined to single cities or at the most to limited areas, such as the Hudson River Steamboat Association. Worsening conditions of competition hastened collective action in all industries with large fixed capital. High capital intensity did not necessarily mean large-scale operation but merely a large investment in plant and equipment in relation to wages and the value of the products. A small distillery, for example, might have fixed capital and wage and income relations similar to a large railroad; a big textile mill might have relatively low fixed capital and wages as its principal factor of cost.

Although Veblen thought that businessmen often inhibited

mergers through placing too high a value on their enterprises, Andrew Carnegie explained how collective action by firms with large invested capital seemed bound to occur.

When an article was produced by a small manufacturer, employing probably at his own home two or three journeymen and an apprentice or two, it was an easy matter for him to limit or stop production. As manufacturing is carried on today, in enormous establishments with five or ten million dollars of capital invested, and with thousands of workers, it costs the manufacturer much less to run at a loss per ton or per yard than to check his production.
The condition of cheap manufacture is running full. Twenty sources of expense are *fixed charges,* many of which stoppage would only increase. Therefore, the article is produced for months, and in some cases that I have known for years, not only without profit or without interest on capital, but to the impairment of the capital invested. . . . His brother manufacturers are of course in the same situation. . . . The manufacturers are in the position of patients that have tried in vain every doctor of the regular school for years, and are now liable to become the victim of any quack that appears. Combinations—syndicates—trusts—they are willing to try anything.[3]

Survival by a combination of independent companies in close association was quite a different solution from merger into a single corporation or trust. A group of small manufacturers, pouring their goods in fixed quotas into a pool, was attempting a method of restriction that would keep the least efficient producer alive. The pool would dispose of the goods at prices sufficient to cover the highest individual costs of production. In the whisky pool, for example, production was apportioned among some eighty distilleries, most of which had relatively high costs.

By using similar devices small business in England and Western Europe was kept alive. But belief in the free market and legal hostility to "restraint of trade" made United States

pools and other price-fixing associations imperfect and un-
reliable. Operating outside the law, pacts to control competition had only the force of "gentlemen's agreements," and
every large group included many who could not be counted
on to behave as gentlemen. Consequently, none of these
manufacturing agreements gave more than temporary relief
from cutthroat competition.

The railroads, whose traffic could be observed by competitors, had somewhat greater success with pooling than manufacturers. By 1880 most of the highly competitive long-haul
traffic was pooled. The Omaha pool of railroads operating
from Chicago west and the Trunk Line Association of the
railroads operating to the east were the most important big
pools, but there were scores of regional agreements between
two or more roads governing competitive routes. The pools
generally set rates and apportioned traffic on the basis of past
performance. If a road then hauled more than its share it
paid a penalty into the pool. Many railroad executives
thought that the solution to the railroad rate situation was
pooling with rates made legally enforceable.

Consolidation into one single company had obvious advantages in legality and efficiency over any of these extra-legal
methods of association. For example, in 1887, when the
whisky distillers agreed to merge into one firm, known euphe-
mistically as the Cattle Feeders and Distillers Corporation,
they were able to close down more than seventy distilleries
and supply the market from the dozen most efficient plants.
But, as Veblen observed, it was hard to bring competitors
together voluntarily, and some big companies such as Standard Oil grew by what might be called conquest. The firm
that first achieved a large scale of operation could produce

each unit more cheaply and make better bargains with the railroads for handling its larger volume of shipments. Thus the leading firm could set prices below the costs of smaller competitors and force them to sell out. On occasion, as both Veblen and Henry Demarest Lloyd noted, these market pressures were re-enforced by threats and violence.

Before 1889, however, the general incorporation acts of the states did not allow companies to hold the stock of other corporations. Therefore, a merger involved either forming a new financial structure or finding some legal way of attaching the bought firm to its new parent. In railroads the solution was for a larger interest to buy the controlling securities of a company and then lease it for a long term, as when the Vanderbilts bought control of the Canada Southern in 1877, and subsequently leased it to their Michigan Central company for ninety-nine years. In manufacturing, where no such long-run stability was visualized, the device of trusteeship was used. The term "trust" technically meant that the shareholders of merged companies put their stock in the hands of a board of trustees and received trust certificates in return. S.C.T. Dodd, the Standard Oil lawyer, is credited with having first applied this system to a corporation in 1879.

In 1889 New Jersey passed a general incorporation act that permitted a company to own the stock of other companies. Ten years later Delaware passed an even more liberal law; the whole operation could be performed without any stockholder of the new corporation taking the trouble to travel to Delaware. The old "trusts," by this time under attack from state and federal courts, soon became "holding companies" with New Jersey or Delaware charters.

By 1890 railroads and some public utilities were already

large companies, and in many places they were also local
monopolies. In manufacturing or processing the size of companies was increasing rapidly, and several trusts had been
formed. Production of refined petroleum and sugar, cotton
and linseed oil, matches, tobacco, whisky, cordage, and lead
were each dominated by a single large firm.[4] These companies varied considerably in the control they could exercise
over their markets and may, *in toto,* seem peripheral to the
main types of production and distribution, but the alarming
thing to contemporary observers like Veblen was that they
had all appeared within about a decade. If the movement
were to continue and to grow it would not be long before
each type of production was monopolized and the worker and
consumer reduced to the status of serfs in an industrial feudalism. This was the possibility that led associations of small
businessmen, farm organizations, and journalists like Henry
Demarest Lloyd to devote their energy to combating the
trusts.

Such pressure was almost irresistible politically, and the
states and the federal government passed anti-trust laws. In
the bold and sweeping language of the Sherman Anti-Trust
Act, passed by Congress in 1890:

Every contract, combination in the form of trust or otherwise, or
conspiracy, in restraint of trade or commerce among the several
states, or with foreign nations, is hereby declared to be illegal. . . .
Every person who shall monopolize, or attempt to monopolize, or
combine or conspire with any other person or persons to monopolize any part of the trade or commerce among the several States, or
with foreign nations, shall be deemed guilty of a misdemeanor. . . .[5]

The law was both a criminal and a civil statute; it provided
for fines and imprisonment, as well as triple damages to in-
jured parties.

Obviously, such a drastic law was partly a gesture by legislators to reassure their farm and business constituents. No big business executive ever went to jail for violation of the Sherman Act. However, its interpretation by the Supreme Court had, by 1911, established certain ground rules for business agreements or mergers. Any agreement among a number of firms to fix prices, or to allot production or territories was illegal, as was any effort, by labor or others, to boycott particular firms. Complete monopoly, unless based on the limited duration of particular patents, was obviously outside the law. The percentage of control of the market that constituted illegal monopoly would be decided by the Court in each case on the basis of the effect of the control on the public interest.

Big companies such as railroads, public utilities, or industrial "trusts" generally raised their capital by public sale of securities. As these companies grew and multiplied, so did the business of marketing securities, carried on by investment bankers. By the 1870s investment banking houses such as Drexel, Morgan; August Belmont; Winslow, Lanier; Lee, Higginson; or Kuhn, Loeb formed a substantial and powerful part of the financial community. To handle railroad issues running into tens of millions of dollars, these houses formed syndicates with each other and with their foreign correspondents. At this time the English and Western European security markets for high-grade bonds were better than United States markets, where new security offerings tended to outrun the available savings. Consequently the strongest American houses were based on reliable foreign outlets. Drexel, Morgan, for example, had its own partners in both London and Paris, as well as close relations with the great English firm of Baring Brothers. Kuhn, Loeb could draw on the resources of the Deutsch Bank of Berlin, while August Belmont and Company represented the ubiquitous Rothschilds.

In a nation hard pressed for funds to meet the needs of a geographically expanding economy, these controllers of the supply of security capital, who were also figures of international importance, became leaders of a new business elite. Like the importing merchants of the colonial period, they knew through their influential overseas connections what was going on in the world, and they could greatly influence what was undertaken by big business. Under such auspices, Veblen thought, the credit system became a form of extensive industrial sabotage.

Although the dozen leading houses were not part of any regularized hierarchy of power, J. Pierpont Morgan, between 1890 and 1913, acted as a *de facto* leader. His influence rested on local resources second to none, strong foreign connections, a dominating personality, and willingness to take responsibility. In 1889, for example, he persuaded the leading investment houses to agree to withhold financing from eastern railroads that cut rates. He called the railroad presidents to his library to announce the rule. He talked, said President Roberts of the Pennsylvania, as though "we, the railroad people, [were] a set of anarchists and this [was] an attempt to substitute law and order for anarchy and might." [6] So influential was Morgan's role in big business and finance that these years around the turn of the century have often been called the "Morgan Era." In no period before or since has the influence of one man been so widely recognized in American business.

Much of the Morgan eminence came from the increasing power of the entire financial community. The big New York banks such as National City Bank or First National and the trust companies such as Bankers and Guarantee were more than ever the shapers of commercial banking policy. National City Bank had a gold reserve rivaling that of the Treasury and held deposits for more than 200 large out-of-town banks. During these years the presidents of the chief New York City banks conferred and cooperated closely with Morgan and other leading investment bankers.

In the nineties life insurance companies became financial giants. The assets of the five largest companies rose from under $400 million in 1890 to about $1.5 billion in 1900.[7] Their annual premium and investment income plus that of dozens of smaller companies offered a major market for new securities. Consequently Morgan and the other leading bankers bought controlling blocks of stock in the big insurance companies and took seats on their boards of directors.

This concentration of financial power in the hands of a few New Yorkers, evident in the panic of 1907, led to a Congressional investigation by the Pujo Committee. Its report, issued just before J. Pierpont Morgan's death in 1913, called him the leader of a "money trust." The aim of the "trust," if it could be said to have any agreed upon aim, was to keep investment finance sound and conservative, to make the overly speculative American security markets safer for the buyers of high-grade bonds. That this could not be accomplished altogether, or that the effort may have discouraged expansion of useful enterprises (Veblen's "sabotage"), could be seen as part of the price that had to be paid for lack of any official central banking system before 1914.

Accompanying the rise of security capitalism was an increase in the number of trust companies to manage estates and financial lawyers to protect the interests of trustees, banks, and corporations. John B. Dill began a lecture at the Harvard Law School with "I am the lawyer for a billion dollars of invested capital." [8] Unfortunately, the census does not show the increase of such occupations. But numbers would be no guide to the great social influence that was wielded by these men who were close, in one way or another, to the allocation and control of capital represented by securities.[9]

While the manipulators of capital and credit occupied the attention of journalists and scholars, the rank and file of American, or for that matter world, businessmen were in small-scale service and trade. By the 1890s the distributing system of the United States had reached maximum complexity, and it is not surprising that Veblen questioned the value of so many middlemen. Commission merchants, brokers, agents, jobbers, and salesmen channeled goods in various ways from producers or importers to wholesalers and retailers. The meaning of each title varied from one activity to another, but most such middlemen avoided the accumulation of a stock of goods, buying, even in carload lots, only for prompt resale. Manufacturers' agents also arranged for delivery of the products from the suppliers they represented directly to wholesalers and retailers without taking possession of the goods. Either hiring salesmen or performing this function themselves, these expediters of marketing could work out of a small office. Wholesalers, on the other hand, bought the goods of many producers and stored them in warehouses for resale over a considerable period, and many agents for nation-wide firms did the same with the products of their particular suppliers.

But signs of a reduction in complexity were already present.

An increasing number of branches staffed by employees of the main firm sold directly, in some cases to individual consumers, in local markets. In the 1880s sales from mail-order catalogues began to grow rapidly. Big companies like Montgomery Ward and Sears Roebuck could deliver goods from their producers by mail, for cash, considerably cheaper than the consumer could buy through the usual marketing channels. Around 1900, chain stores such as Woolworth and A. & P. appeared. In each case smaller retailers found ways of keeping alive by more efficient arrangements for supply, and by offering service and credit.

Advertising was at least as old as American business, but until the 1840s it had always been held back by the high cost of paper and printing and the local character of most markets. By 1870 rotary presses and sulfite-process pulp paper made magazine and newspaper space cheap enough for lavish display, and firms trying to capture a national market for their brands began extensive advertising. Most firms, however regarded advertising as a minor department until at least the 1890s, and advertising men were treated with condescension or suspicion, as smacking of show business, huckstering, and slightly dishonest ways of attracting patronage.

From 1890 to 1900, while Veblen was collecting material for *The Theory of Business Enterprise,* advertising expenditures grew rapidly, and its agencies and specialists became respected members of the business community. Agencies hired artists and consulted psychologists, while popular magazines became for business primarily advertising media. Trolleys, elevateds, subways, and suburban trains made car cards important, and the bicycle and automobile gave new life to outdoor advertising. By 1910 the total of advertising expenditure reached 4 per cent of the national income, a figure never substantially exceeded.[10]

Advertising knit the business community more tightly together. By appealing directly to consumers through advertising a manufacturer could force wholesalers and retailers to carry his product. Supplying most of the revenue for newspapers and magazines, large advertisers exerted power for considerate treatment in the field of publishing and, in general, made the media conservative, cautious, and nonpartisan. Through trade associations, the advertising agencies and the media added their influence to many others that were bringing local businessmen together in weekly or monthly meetings, partly social and partly business. Basically, appeals developed by advertising experts tended to crystallize the myths and values of high-level consumption. The appeals aimed at inflating marketing slogans or attitudes into stronger forces for educating and conditioning the public. For example, the ultimate desirability of a Packard, and of the largest one rather than the smallest, was a lesson in values more readily learned by the young man of the early 1900s than the desirability of intelligent participation in local politics.

From recognition of this aspect of advertising, public relations was emerging as a professional technique. Building favorable opinion for an industry or a firm, without emphasis on selling a particular product, had beginnings in the United States. Publisher's agents in the 1840s, iron, steel, and wool association lobbyists in the 1850s, railroad executives after the Civil War, and electric traction and utility representatives at the end of the century all helped establish the field. By the first decade of the new century "publicity agencies," as distinct from advertising agencies, began to appear. Among these pioneers the work of Ivy Lee for the Telephone Company, the Pennsylvania Railroad, and the Rockefeller interests was the most notable.

With improved transport and with machine industry, the nonagricultural business population increased rapidly, and the proprietors, partners, managers, and administrators of commercially oriented firms, according to Veblen, created a pecuniary culture in towns and cities. In each decade, from at least 1820, the total personal influence of businessmen must have grown. Increasing opportunity in nonagricultural business accords with the general structure of developing industrialism. A few hundred firms in a score or more of highly capitalized industries became big and semi-monopolistic. Thousands of new firms started each year either in the many lines of manufacturing continually opened up by new technology or in the much larger areas of trade and service that arose from increasing levels of consumption. If one thinks of American businessmen in point of numbers rather than in terms of power or wealth, they have always been best represented by retailers. All other groups of firms are small compared to the number of stores of all types and sizes.

Like other Americans the small enterprisers, equaling perhaps 6 per cent of all gainful workers in 1890, were a mobile population. Of firms listed by Dun and Bradstreet, which were presumably larger and more stable than the unlisted remainder, about 10 per cent failed in the average year between 1870 and 1910, and 16 per cent failed in the depression year of 1878. Failure usually did not mean an end to the proprietor's entrepreneurial activity, but merely that he reopened in a new area, or became an employee for a time until he found a new opportunity. According to these average figures, the firm with the same name, proprietor, and location that was five years old would be the exception, as would be the middle western farmer who was still on the same farm.

This mobility was caused partly by the continual settlement of new communities that promised less competitive markets than the older towns. Merle E. Curti notes in his frontier Trempealeau County, Wisconsin: "Only a very small number of the non-agriculturally employed stayed from 1860 to 1870." [11] Most of the businessmen for whom information was available in Trempealeau County formed partnerships; "many partnerships, however, were short lived." [12]

These businessmen plus many of the better paid white collar workers and highly skilled operatives as well as the professional people composed the middle and upper classes of the growing town or city. These groups could be regarded as unconsciously probusiness in values and outlook. As Veblen saw it, the small-town pecuniary training perverted the instinct for workmanship. In one sense, as we have seen, this did not differentiate small-town people from other Americans, but it did mean that in labor strikes or disputes the middle class could generally be counted on to support business values.

Veblen had an ambiguous attitude toward the hired executives of large corporations. Since they did not work for their own profit and were advanced on the basis of skill, they were part of the "industrial arts" or of the technicians whose "essential matter-of-factness" would make business obsolete. On the other hand, they made many of the decisions regarding prices, innovation, and control of markets that Veblen regarded as business sabotage.

The growth in power of these professional managers

through the separation of ownership from control had gone on from the start in banking and in some other corporations with widely held stock. These early companies had not developed the physical bigness that makes a corporation permanently employing thousands of men an organization one that cannot be understood or meddled with by an uninformed outsider, even though he may be a member of the board of directors. For example, in 1846 John Murray Forbes of Boston thought he could run the Michigan Central Railroad by studying its problems in his spare time. He soon found the presidency a full-time job and passed it on to a career executive.

The growth in power of railroad managers in relation to their boards of directors in the late nineteenth century was not due to lack of ability among directors to enforce their views, as was to become the case in the twentieth century, but rather to the capitalist's lack of knowledge necessary to make decisions. And the stockholders, of course, were far less informed or able to act than the directors. As a result, managerial enterprise, the control of policy by the salaried officers of the companies rather than by the representatives of ownership, became the rule in railroading in the nineteenth century.

It is a mark of the persistence of institutions, however, that while in day-to-day decision-making the managers exercised the real power, in formal communication they acted their part as the directors' hired men, bound by the wishes of the representatives of ownership. There was, in this period, to be sure, more need than later for managerial ambiguity or circumspection in dealing with directors since certain board members might control the supplies of capital necessary for the expansion of the enterprise. From the 1880s, these men of financial power, such as Forbes, Erastus Corning, or Cornelius or William Vanderbilt, were replaced on railroad boards by the equally powerful representatives of investment banking houses.

Veblen was correct in seeing the rising group of professional managers, the men of the "industrial arts," as socially different from his conception of businessmen. He felt that ultimately these "matter-of-fact" technologically oriented men would take over control of production, and to a degree they did, although not in quite the way Veblen imagined; however, it is worthwhile to examine carefully the characteristics of this social type. One important characteristic was that careerists who succeeded were unusually well educated. Between 1850 and 1890, the percentage of the population eighteen to twenty-one years old who were still in school increased only from 1 to 3 per cent. Of this small group, many must have entered the ministry or become teachers, leaving few college graduates among the farming and business population. Yet all studies of the executives of big corporations in this period indicate that about 40 per cent had attended college. It must be remembered that in the days when college education was limited to a small elite, the friends made there could be of more lasting benefit than the knowledge acquired.

Social connections undoubtedly helped the career executive in a number of ways. To begin with a "good" home background gave the young man a command of the language and a degree of social grace that helped win approval from his superiors and respect from his subordinates. As President Charles Perkins of the Burlington Lines wrote to a general manager in 1886, "It is a great deal better to get in young men of education and good bringing up than it is to trust merely to luck. . . . New England is full of youngsters of good abilities and good characters." [13] In a big organization, knowledge of the existence of a young man by men in the top echelon of management because of his personal connections was often a first step in getting ahead. The young man who was "socially" known or wore the old school tie had a visibility that could only be acquired by others through hard work or good luck. Occasionally family connections might directly influence decision for promotion, but good managers tried to resist such pressures.[14]

As Veblen foresaw, these well-educated professionals, administering other people's money, gradually developed a new code of corporate ethics and a new role for themselves in society. In the beginning railroad executives acted as though they were still individual proprietors. As dealers, they sold supplies to the railroad companies whose policies they controlled. They advanced their private capital to companies for construction, and charged the railroad high prices payable in stocks and bonds. They owned bridges and equipment and rented them at exorbitant rates to the roads. They profited greatly as real estate operators from an inside knowledge of where stations and shops were to be located.

The major period of the development of the modern code of ethics governing relationships between railroad management and stockholders was from the 1860s to the 1880s. In 1860 even the most scrupulous directors or officers were still to be found on both sides of bargains. John W. Brooks, an able, and, by the corporate standards of the day, a strictly honest railroad president, wrote to James F. Joy in 1861: "I suppose

Hall has told you all about our plans for getting the Lewiston road built by which you and I and Ward can share in the spoils." [15] In the increasingly strict ethical atmosphere of the 1870s, favors tended to be reduced to giving the insiders the business at the market price. President James M. Walker of the Burlington wrote to director Brooks asking that the latter's Union Coal Company "reduce the cost . . . to the lowest possible figure," adding: "We shall not fail to go as far as we can to promote the interests of the Union—taking care at the same time that . . . we do no injury to the C.B. & Q.R.R." [16]

By the middle 1880s fiduciary obligations to the stockholders were coming to be recognized by scrupulous executives in a well-defined form that was to be a lasting, although not always observed, pattern. Perkins wrote in 1885 to a vice-president: "The smallest kind of interest in a coal mine would be objectionable. . . . It is against my principles to be interested in any industry of this kind on the line of the road." [17] A little later Henry B. Ledyard of the Michigan Central wrote that he had "long since made it a rule not to have any pecuniary interest in any company or corporation which has any arrangements whatever with the [railroad] company." [18]

Extension of the code to include dealings with customers and the public welfare was more gradual, and only partially achieved before World War I. There was, and apparently always has been, a tendency to identify the welfare of company and community. Even as philosophical a thinker as Forbes observed that "whatever rates of fare and speed are best for the road are best for its surrounding country." [19] Dealings with customers were assumed to follow the inexorable laws of the market, but these laws also seemed to include those of monopoly pricing. William H. Osborn, president of the Illinois Central, complained in 1863 that the railroads of New York State took the "spoils of the products of the prairies, seven-eighths to forwarders, and one-eighth to the poor devil that raises the corn." [20] As Perkins saw it: "The business of a railroad freight agent must keep many considerations in mind." Perkins believed, in general, that the value added to the product by transportation should determine what it could bear in rates.[21] Judged merely by the preponderance of opinion expressed in some railroad correspondence it appears that presidents supported the Veblenian idea of business. They saw it as a device for achieving scarcity by regarding moderately high rates with less traffic as a safer road to profits than expanded traffic with lower rates. There is no similar body of opinion by executives in any other "managerial" industry (strictly, there was no other), but the railroad case makes it appear that the twentieth century view of cutting price to expand the market, as distinguished from cutting to eliminate competitors, was not well regarded by professional management in the nineteenth century. Big shippers who could divide their business between two or more roads could bargain for special rates. While this practice was deplored by the railroadmen, since such special rates or rebates from the posted rates were the result of competition in the market, it was not regarded as unethical.[22]

In giving money or services for community purposes professional managers interpreted their obligations to the stockholders with varying degrees of breadth. If the contribution or service was directly in the interest of economic development it could readily be seen as a long-run aid to profits.

Perkins, for example, felt justified in giving $5,000 of his stockholder's money to a fair at Lincoln, Nebraska, because "it would pay us to help out in all such public matters as this on general principle." [23] Thomas F. Oakes, later president of the Northern Pacific, claimed that at one time he "found it necessary to feed an entire community for three months and carry provisions free of charge for six months." [24] Acutely conscious of the importance of entrepreneurship in economic growth, railroad executives took a paternal interest in businessmen along the line. Frederick J. Kimball of the Norfolk and Western, for example, wrote one of his subordinates: "Norfolk has not grown in importance to the extent one would expect. I think it would be very well for you to spend considerable time there with the merchants." [25] Thus the longer time horizons of the big-company administrator produced an increasing degree of social responsibility in their "technological" behavior.

Limited use of the stockholder's money was also justifiable for support in those organizations that preserved social stability or improved the performance of workers. But the railroad executive should not make any contributions that could more properly be made by the stockholders as individuals. Brooks appears to have expressed the prevailing corporate code when he wrote:

Our mission is not that of aiding institutions of learning or religion because they may commend themselves to our personal judgment . . . . We can properly help. . . . When it is clearly for the pecuniary advantage of our stockholders that we should do so, as for instance, if it would raise the price of adjacent land belonging to the company we could make a donation of land for the location of an educational institution. [26]

In practice, this rather narrow view of the interest of the stockholders was generally expanded to include the building of a good public image of the company, if the cost was low. Free or reduced fare transportation was given to ministers, editors, and some educators. Brooks explained these expenditures, hard to relate directly to profit, by saying: "I suppose we must do what will make people feel that we are decent . . . and keep our line right with the general public." [27] Following the same reasoning, President William K. Ackerman would endow a room in a hospital only if it were called the Illinois Central Room. "Unless we can have this I do not see any particular advantage in making the endowment." [28] Aside from company service, the newspaper was the continual media for creating the corporate image, and the friendship of editors was of major importance. President Watrous of the New York, New Haven, and Hartford, wrote an editor: "We care less about making profit (if we can perform the service without actual loss) than about aiding in a general and prompt dissemination of the news." [29]

Between 1890 and 1903, when *The Theory of Business Enterprise* went to Scribner's, a number of industrial and public utility corporations and a few banks and insurance companies joined the railroads in the ranks of managerially run big business. The total of all types of managerial enterprises was certainly well under a thousand companies, and their policy-forming officers well under 100,000 men. Yet this small group of professional executives represented the most important emerging force in American business, a group that seemed destined to grow steadily in numbers and power. Hence the evolution of the managerial social role, as a force in society and as a device for reflecting outside social pres-

sures inside the corporation, was of great potential importance. Even by the first decade of the twentieth century, the
men most active in national affairs were likely to have this
background. George W. Perkins, of United States Steel,
Robert de Forrest of Jersey Central, Edward H. Harriman of
the western railroads, Frank Vanderlip of National City
Bank, and scores of other men whose influence was strongly
felt in political and civic affairs had risen by the professional
career ladder, even though some of them had amassed considerable private wealth in the process.

The uniformities of the executive role tended to give these
men certain qualities less common in the older types of American businessmen. They were accustomed to calculating broad
effects in the remote future with a calculus that integrated
other factors with pecuniary gain. They realized that their
actions could affect both politics and society, and that they
had to have an interest in each. They favored special education and expert knowledge, in contrast to the antagonism
most businessmen felt toward theorists and college graduates.
They cultivated an objective view of business situations in
which company welfare was expected to supersede personal
desires. In short, they represented an emerging institutional,
status-oriented type of capitalism in contrast to the individual, market-oriented type of earlier centuries.

A new availability of capital and a new emphasis on increasing mass consumption accompanied this shift in the
dominant business role. The transition during the twentieth
century led to basic alterations in the managerial capitalist
ethic difficult to foresee in Veblen's time. Interpreting Veblen
rather broadly, we could hold that these men represented in
their early careers, at least, the "industrial arts" and over-

came the transitional style of capitalism, as Veblen predicted they would. Unpredicted, however, was the failure of the "matter-of-fact" professionals in big business to end capitalism in that sector. On the other hand, small business, with its more directly pecuniary aims, did not go broke but continued to thrive.

The Sacred and the Profane: The Theology of Thorstein Veblen

David W. Noble

My RESEARCH has always shown a concern with the role of primitivism in the imagination of modern society. As an undergraduate I had learned that a new kind of liberalism, pragmatic and realistic, rooted in an acceptance of evolution and the inevitability of historical change, had appeared in the United States during the first decade of the twentieth century. But when I attempted to analyze the controlling assumptions of the *New Republic* magazine, which had been founded in 1914 explicitly as the voice for this new liberalism, I discovered that the editors of this "realistic and pragmatic" journal had expected something very much like the millennium to appear between 1914 and 1917 and were, therefore, completely confused by 1919 as to the meaning of social evolution and the historical process.[1]

I became curious about the philosophic pattern of the new liberalism of the progressive period, which proclaimed allegiance to a theory of unending historical change but seemed to anticipate an apocalyptic end to history in the immediate future. As I began to study a number of the important liberal social philosophers of that period, I became convinced that a major paradox rested at the foundation of their outlook. Most of these men seemed to be arguing that the new urban-industrial society, emerging at the end of the nineteenth century, marked the end of the historical civilization which had appeared five thousand years before in the Near East. From 3000 B.C. to A.D. 1900 humanity, according to this new liberalism, had lived in a world of dreadful war and competition, but now industrialism was making it possible for mankind to dwell in the kind of close-knit and productive community which had characterized primitive man. The liberal social philosophers of 1900 postulated that prehistoric man was by nature altruistic and gregarious and that the patterns of war and competition of historical civilization had been imposed by the false traditions and institutions of the artificial cultures which had so obscured the true biological nature of man for these many centuries. The hopeful social philosophers of 1900 then prophesied that industrialism was destroying every evil historical institution and tradition and liberating the good instincts of the natural man. Industrial progress meant a return to a primitive Utopia.[2]

Since these twentieth-century liberals so clearly wanted civilization to be purged and purified in a return to an earlier and more virtuous state of simplicity and since they described the corrupt society of their day by evoking the imagery of medieval civilization, I began to consider the possibility that the imagination of these latter-day Puritans might be related to the imagination of the first Puritans of 1600. And when one analyzes the outlook of the seventeenth-century

Puritans, one becomes aware of certain massive parallels with
the Puritans of the early twentieth century. The earlier Puritans condemned the civilization of their day because it was
artificial and, therefore, corrupt. They too prophesied the
destruction of the institutions and traditions of the historical
past which would allow the emancipated individual to return
to a state of primitive simplicity. For these Puritans of 1600,
of course, that first perfection was the true church as God had
willed its existence. This prehistoric church might, however,
be described as natural because it was not a man-made institution, and it incorporated no man-made traditions. This, the
Puritans had proclaimed, was the great curse of the medieval
church of Roman Catholicism. It was a man-made institution
which did incorporate man-made traditions.

And so the Puritans of the seventeenth century rebelled
against this historical church in the hope of returning to the
prehistoric church. For these purifiers, there could be no
meaningful reform of any human institution or tradition. For
them, salvation depended upon a return to the timelessness of
God's original creation. Purification meant the destruction of
every profane human creation in order to achieve harmony
with the sacred world of divine origin.

Faced with what seemed to be a fanatical religious primitivism in 1600 as well as 1900, I began to take this theological
hostility to civilization so seriously that I asked the question:
If a major ideological theme in modern times has been a
hostility to the idea of civilization, is it possible that many
modern men, inspired by the vision of a prehistorical Eden,
actually have returned to the imagination of prehistoric man
himself? I began to read in the history of early religions and,
by chance, happened upon the books of Mircea Eliade,

Cosmos and History and *The Sacred and the Profane*. In Eliade's analysis, the terms sacred and profane are central to the understanding of the religious imagination of primitive men. For them the world of time and space is either sacred or profane. Sacred time and space are the direct expression of the creativity of the gods. Sacred space is that area which has been stamped with a divinely harmonious pattern that distinguishes it from the chaos, the formlessness of profane space. "Sacred time," Eliade writes, "is a mythical time, that is, a primordial time, not to be found in the historical past, an original time, in the sense that it came into existence all at once, that it was not preceded by another time, because no time could exist before the appearance of the reality narrated in the myth." And, Eliade continues:

Since the sacred and strong time is the time of origins, the stupendous instant in which a reality was created, was for the first time fully manifested, [primitive] man will seek periodically to return to that original time . . . [because for primitive man] life cannot be repaired, it can only be recreated through symbolic repetition of the cosmogony, for, as we have said, the cosmogony is the paradigmatic model for all creation. [The prehistoric man] desires to live in the world as it came from the Creator's hands, fresh, pure, and strong . . . [because] what men do on their own initiative, what they do without a mythical model, belongs to the sphere of the profane; hence it is a vain and illusory activity and, in the last analysis, unreal.[3]

I am going to argue then that in their revolt against medieval civilization, against all civilization, the Puritans of 1600 defined civilization as a profane creation of human initiative, as "a vain and illusory activity and, in the last analysis, unreal." I am going to argue that the Puritans reintroduced as a major theme in modern culture "the myth of the Eternal

Return," the belief in the possibility of destroying profane time and returning to the sacred time of origin. And I am going to argue that Thorstein Veblen, as a representative American social philosopher of 1900, was a major Puritan prophet who first had to demonstrate that the seventeenth-century Puritans had failed to destroy profane civilization, but that now the beginning of the twentieth century was indeed a progressive era. Profane time would be purged and man would be liberated to return to the sacred time "as it came from the Creator's hands, fresh, pure, and strong."

Scholars have usually interpreted Veblen as a rebel and a radical. They have described him as an enemy of the *status quo* and as a spokesman for change and innovation. But one is immediately struck by Veblen's absolute rejection of the possibility of reform or even revolution. For him the only possible salvation of society lay in the destruction of all man-made institutions and traditions, a purification of the profane which would permit the restoration of a sacred time of origin. Veblen launched his attack on his scholarly colleagues who argued that the American *status quo* was natural and, there-fore, sacred and that any attempt to destroy the existing situation would force man into the terrors of profane history.

The conservatives defined themselves as protectors of a suc-cessful Puritan revolution which had destroyed the profane and restored the sacred. Once, they explained, men had lived in bondage to the profane, man-made institutions and tradi-tions of medieval civilization. And they had lived within the terror of historical chaos. But the Puritans of the seventeenth century had rebelled against the feudal aristocracy and the priestly class which prospered through their parasitical ex-ploitation of the people. These they kept subdued by armed force and the fear of the superstitions with which they had inculcated the innocent citizenry.

The seventeenth-century Puritans, however, had rallied the common man in rebellion against the parasitical privileged classes in the name of the right of each individual to find truth outside institutions and traditions. Each individual could find truth by reading the original revelation of God in the Bible. Here it was revealed that God wanted the individual to serve Him directly through his productive economic calling.

As one moved from the seventeenth to the eighteenth century, however, religious Puritanism gave way to secular Puritanism which prophesied that through science an even more reliable revelation of God's will was to be found in the natural law of God's physical creation than in the Bible. Since it was now demonstrated by science that this physical creation was one of perfect harmony as contrasted with the total chaos of man-made society, the reverent individual would model his economic activity on natural law. And since God held the distinct atoms of the physical universe in constant harmony with one another, it followed that each individual operating as an atom of economic self-interest would necessarily work in conjunction with and not conflict with other individuals. The autonomous enjoyment of private property by the self-sufficient and self-reliant individual was defined as a return to the sacred time of origin, to the authentic and harmonious world of nature as God had created it. This was in opposition to the profane and chaotic society of medieval civilization when the individual had been forced away from his commitment to the God-given to be a slave to the man-made.

As the nineteenth century began, the capitalist, as one who

had escaped from the profane time of artificially contrived
institutions and traditions, had the responsibility to preserve
this sacred organic unity with the laws of nature. The capitalist, as Puritan, must not allow the dragon of chaos to seduce
his people back into the disorder of profane historical man-
made civilization, back into medieval blackness. The law of
laissez-faire must be defended at all costs because it was a
reflection of the original order of the universe. Socialism then
was the doctrine of the dragon of chaos because it wanted to
substitute a transitory and a human for an eternal and divine
way of life.

In 1890, however, Thorstein Veblen declared himself a
socialist and set out to prove that the capitalist was the real
dragon of chaos and the socialist was the true communicant
of the sacred time of origins. And if Veblen was right then, of
course, no Puritan revolution had occurred in the seventeenth and eighteenth centuries which had destroyed medieval civilization and had fulfilled the myth of the Eternal
Return. If Veblen was right, a Puritan revolution must now
occur which would destroy historical civilization and restore
mankind to the state of nature, to the sacred time of origin.

One of the major thrusts of Veblen's intellectual energy in
the 1890s then was to prove that capitalism was not natural
and that the economists who defended it were not scientific.
Since Veblen attempts to discredit his capitalist opponents on
the grounds that they are men of faith, a man-made faith
which put them in bondage to the mysteries of a belief in a
spiritual reality beyond the brute facts of material existence,
it may seem confusing for me to argue that this is strong evidence of Veblen's loyalty to a primitive religious outlook.
Indeed, most students of Veblen's thought have stressed the

severely materialistic and, therefore, secular nature of his imagination.

But let us return to Eliade's description of the primitive religious imagination. For Eliade the primitive man is not self-conscious of having a faith. He believes that he knows empirically what the gods created, and his act of reverence is to imitate that creation in empirical detail. The primitive man believes he is most sacred when he is in organic harmony with the physical structure that the gods have made. His religious self-consciousness is the absolute antithesis of a self-conscious mysticism. Eliade writes:

For religious man of the primitive and archaic societies, the eternal repetition of the paradigmatic gestures and the eternal recovery of the time of origin . . . in no sense implies a pessimistic vision of life. On the contrary, for him, it is by virtue of this eternal return to the sources of the sacred and the real that human existence appears to be saved from nothingness and death.[4]

Quite clearly, as we shall see, Veblen assumes that his readers are religiously committed to the necessity of an organic relation of the sacred and the real and find inspiration in the possibility of restoring the endless repetition of the paradigm of productivity which characterized the time of origin.

Veblen began his muckraking of modern capitalism, contending that its pretense to sacred harmony was a shallow façade for the profane chaos that was its real character, with an analysis of the seventeenth century. The capitalistic apologists of 1900 described this century as the time when modern man liberated himself from the mysticism, the profane human imagination of medieval darkness, and when the age of modern enlightenment, of scientific empiricism, became dominant. But, declared Veblen, such a reading of scientific and economic history was nonsense. Central to these supposedly modern centuries from 1700 to 1900 has been the faith in progress; and this faith, like all ethereal faiths, could not be empirically demonstrated. No modern scientists, therefore, until Darwin, have been willing to accept a fact as a fact; they all wanted to associate reality with abstract moral values. This was the context for Veblen's article, "Why Is Economics Not an Evolutionary Science?" [5] Nineteenth-century economists, he wrote, thought they were scientific because they called for a realistic examination of the facts of economic life. Accuracy and observation, objectivity and induction were their watchwords. But, without exception, their detailed knowledge was always put into an irrelevant mystical form, because the end they always served was the establishment of an absolute spiritual truth. These scientists of the culture of capitalistic Puritanism shared, therefore, the irrational faith of the Dark Ages that nature acted as if it had propensities and will power. Capitalistic scientists believed that animistic nature was striving to move along the path of progress. In three articles on "The Preconceptions of Economic Science," [6] Veblen developed a detailed historical context to prove that he was the first post-Darwinian economist.

He began by exploring the writings of the Physiocrats and Adam Smith in order to reveal their commitment to a teleology founded on a faith in divine guidance. Veblen rejoiced in reporting that the English economists, John Stuart Mill, and then Marshall and Cairnes had significantly reduced the heritage of animism from the eighteenth century. Nevertheless, he warned, this trend toward mathematical objectivity had not brought economics to the level of a true science. Cairnes and Marshall, perhaps, had rid economics of the besetting sin of animism, but they had not escaped the institutional framework evolved for the expression of that animism. They rejected laws of progress, but they postulated the existence of abstract, artificial laws. And they forced living experience within the framework of these hypothetical laws. They had done everything to make economics into a science except to relate it to reality in the form of matter-of-fact events. For Veblen, then, they had refused to put their economics in organic harmony with "the world as it came from the Creator's hands, fresh, pure, and strong." Instead they worked with man-made models that belonged "to the sphere of the profane; hence it is a vain and illusory activity and, in the last analysis, unreal."

After destroying the objectivity of the English apologists for capitalistic progress, Veblen, the socialist, turned to an even more savage attack on that other prophet of economic progress, Karl Marx. Ruthlessly, he tried to undermine Marx as a rational thinker. With great care, he placed Marx in perspective for his readers as a self-contained and highly original theoretician. "Except as a whole and except in the light of its postulates and aims, the Marxian system is not only not tenable, but it is not even intelligible. . . . There is no system of economic theory more logical than that of Marx." [7] Marx, Veblen contended, stood or fell with his system as a whole; he could not be criticized in detail. But what of this logical masterpiece and what of its postulates? It was a house of cards constructed of pure irrelevancies, Veblen declared; it rested on two metaphysical traditions, the natural-rights liberal school of economists and Hegelian romanticism.

From Hegel, Marx borrowed the idea of progress, necessary progress, culminating in the classless society. From the Eng-

lish, he took his concept of the exploitation of labor by capital and the laborer's claim to the whole product of his labor.
He merged the Hegelian notion of a mysterious, upward
movement through conflict, expressed by a necessary triadic
scheme of thesis, antithesis, and synthesis, with an English-
utilitarian view of psychology. There was nothing really
materialistic about Marx's theory of the class struggle, Veblen
declared; this class struggle was motivated by conscious self-
interest. "It is in fact a piece of hedonism and is related to
Bentham rather than to Hegel." [8]

Veblen, therefore, presented himself to his readers as the
only economist whom they could trust. He, alone, could reveal the truth to his Puritan audience which was loyal to the
Puritan values of scientific empiricism and economic productivity, to the value of individual independence from the corrupting influence of profane traditions and institutions. He
then was the solitary Puritan muckraker who had the awful
responsibility of revealing to the Puritan people that they
were the victims of a vast scholarly conspiracy which had
falsified the records of history and had so deluded the people
that they believed that medieval civilization had been destroyed three hundred years before.

But the truth, said Veblen, was that the culture of the dark
ages still survived and provided the values for the aristocracy
which dominated the United States in 1900, dominated it
economically, politically, socially, and intellectually. One of
Veblen's first articles in the 1890s had been an attack on that
greatest apologist for the capitalist *status quo,* Herbert Spencer. The Englishman had outlined the story of human progress as the escape of man from the irrational system of status
of primitive society to the rational contracts of modern capi-

talism. Under the burden of status no man had been independent. But, for Spencer, each man under the law of free capitalistic contract was autonomous and self-sufficient. Veblen categorically contradicted this reading of history. Capitalism, Veblen asserted, was a system of status where every man was a slave to social patterns; where every man was the prisoner of the dragon of chaos; where no man was in harmony with the natural harmony of the time of origin. And he set out to prove this in his first book, *The Theory of the Leisure Class.*

Veblen began his education of the American Puritan public with a simple definition of the leisure class. "This class," he wrote, "emerged gradually during the transition from primitive savagery to barbarism . . . during the transition from a peaceable to a consistently warlike habit of life." [9] This class, he continued, despises peaceful productivity and industry and loves warlike exploitation. Here in America, as in western Europe, the extremely warlike stage of barbarism has given way to a quasi-peaceable stage "whose characteristic feature is a formal observance of peace and order" but which "still has too much of coercion and class antagonism to be called peaceable." This is "the age of status." [10]

Veblen suggested that we modern Puritans, while shocked to discover that such a feudal class still existed, must recognize that "the best development" of the leisure class "lies in the past rather than in the present." The basic economic pattern of the nineteenth century is rational industrial productivity, which is completely contradictory to the parasitical values of conspicuous consumption characterizing the feudal leisure class. And this new evolutionary economic force must ultimately destroy this obsolete culture: "The evolution of society is substantially a process of mental adaption on the part of individuals under the stress of circumstances which will no longer tolerate habits of thought formed under and conforming to a different set of circumstances in the past." [11] While "the collective interests of any modern community center in industrial efficiency," these "industrial virtues—that is to say, the peaceable traits," are found "chiefly among the classes given to mechanical industry." And the leisure class, removed from the honest productivity of industrialism, therefore, preserves its "aristocratic and bourgeois virtues—that is to say, the destructive and pecuniary traits." [12]

At first glance, Veblen continued, one might worry about the cultural lag which allows this leisure class to be isolated from the economic forces making for fruitful change because the "tendency of the institution of a leisure class in shaping human character runs in the direction of spiritual . . . reversion. Its effect upon the temper of a community is of the nature of an arrested spiritual development." [13] The leisure class, because it controls the press, the pulpit, and the professors, tempts the productive and puritanical common man with its values of conspicuous waste. But, for Veblen, there was no strong reality in all this establishment of the idle rich; there was no power in its professors or priests or politicians because they only controlled man-made institutions. This establishment was that which Eliade described as "what men do on their own initiative [and] what they do without a mythical model [belonging] to the sphere of the profane; hence it is a vain and illusory activity, and, in the last analysis, unreal."

The great gospel of hope that Veblen now held out for the Puritan workers was that industrialism would inevitably destroy this artificial leisure class and, in so doing, liberate the people to return to the time of origin. For Veblen it was good news to preach that "life cannot be repaired, it can only be recreated through symbolic repetition of the cosmogony" because "the sacred and strong time is the time of origins, the stupendous instant in which a reality was created." For Veblen, all American Puritans desire "to live in the world as it came from the Creator's hands, fresh, pure and strong."

The logic of industrialism, Veblen wrote, is to encourage productivity and peacefulness, and these traits are those of the primitive community which preceded the stages of barbarism. As Veblen described the coming destruction of profane time and the restoration of sacred time, one must again note the nature of this sacred time of origin as described by Eliade: "It neither changes nor is it exhausted." This changeless natural reality of primitive productive and peaceful savagery had, in Veblen's description, survived the superficial chaos imposed by the changeful and ephemeral institutional and traditional patterns of barbarism. "The barbarian culture," Veblen wrote, "has been neither protracted enough nor invariable enough in character to give an extreme fixity of type." [14] There was, he insisted, an original biological nature of man, peaceful and productive. When man is liberated by industrialism, his departures "from the human nature of the hereditary present are most frequently of the nature of reversion to an earlier . . . temperament which characterizes the primitive phase of peaceable savagery." Industrialism, as Veblen described it, was a new infusion of reality which was conquering the dragon of chaos and allowing men to once again live by their true natures, which were in spiritual harmony with both the original reality and its new form of expression

in the machine process. There was, Veblen wrote, a "non-
invidious residue of religious life" in all men, "the sense of
communion with the environment, or with the generic life
process." And these, "as well as the impulse of charity and
sociability, act in a pervasive way to shape men's habits of
thought for the economic purpose." [15]

The Puritan people had no need to fear the future because
the force of industrialism must inevitably restore the timeless
peace and harmony of savagery when men lived in perfect
spiritual harmony with the eternal and immutable laws of
nature. The people did not have the responsibility of fighting
the dragon of chaos as Marx had claimed.

Industrialism was, of course, first freeing the productive
workers from intellectual bondage to the barbarian values of
status.

These habits and views begin to lose their coercive force for the
community . . . so soon as the habit of minds . . . due to the
predatory . . . discipline cease to be in fairly close accord with the
later-developed economic situation. This is evident in the case of
the industrious classes of modern communities; for them the leisure-
class scheme of life has lost much of its binding force, especially as
regards the element of status.[16]

Veblen's prophecy became still more optimistic when he
looked at the leisure class itself. Its members were the most
indoctrinated by barbarism, and, for Veblen, they had to an
extent even suffered a biological change, making them by instinct predatory, and thus separating them from the instinctive altruism of the original human type. But in the largest
measure they had retained this first genetic structure, and
their barbarism was basically still only cultural conditioning.
Even in their insulation from the productive process of indus-

trialism, this latest stage of the leisure class was more peaceful than earlier barbaric stages. War was sublimated as sport, dominance as conspicuous consumption. The drift of the leisure class, therefore, was itself away from the violence of barbarism back toward the Eden of savagery.

And, Veblen argued, the leisure class could not continue to escape the impact of industrialism, becoming increasingly the dominant economic and moral force for the entire community. It was infiltrating the leisure class and allying itself with the already developing momentum of peaceful tendencies of the aristocracy. Among the women and the priests of the elite there were dramatic signs of rebellion against predatory values and a return to the ultimate ethics of primitive altruism. Most important, however, for Veblen was the change in education. Formerly the educational leaders had defended the barbaric *status quo* by making learning part of the pattern of conspicuous waste. But now "since the relation of mastery and subservience is ceasing to be the dominant and formative factor in the community's life process, other features of the life process and other points of view are forcing themselves upon the scholars." [17] Gradually, the universities were turning from the "archaism and waste" of classical education to incorporate the practical scientific pursuits which had been created by industrialism.

Eliade describes the primitive religious imagination as also visualizing a dichotomy between profane and sacred space. Profane space is space dominated by the primordial dragon, symbolizing chaos. Sacred space is space defined and ordered by the gods. When primitive man conquered a new area, he assumed that he was repeating the pattern of divine order originally imposed upon chaotic profane space by the gods.

And he assumed that the houses he built and his cities also repeated the initial pattern of the sacred order. "A creation implies a superabundance of reality, in other words an irruption of the sacred into the world. It follows that every construction or fabrication has the cosmogony as paradigmatic model. The creation of the world becomes the archetype of every creative human gesture."

In Veblen's version of the religion of the sacred and the profane the prehistorical Eden had been universal. All space had been made harmoniously sacred and all men lived in the timeless perfection of sacred time. But somehow the dragon of chaos had been able to drive all men into the disharmony of the profane time of barbarism. Physical nature remained in a state of sacred order, but men now lived in the artificial and profane space of barbaric culture with its chaotic and disharmonious institutions and traditions. And then about 1600 a miracle began to occur, a new irruption of the sacred into the world which was destined to destroy the dragon of chaos. In England man had remained closer to the sacredness of physical nature because the artificial space of medieval civilization was not so completely imposed upon the isolated island as it was upon the European continent. English Puritans began to regain a vision of the time of origin when man was productive and not parasitical. Gradually, throughout the seventeenth and eighteenth centuries, Englishmen had struggled against the invidious values of the medieval leisure class to regain the original paradigm of honest workmanship.

This drama of the fall from Eden and of the progressive pilgrimage of Puritanism for the last three centuries to return to the sacred time and space of primitivism was recounted in Veblen's second book, *The Theory of Business Enterprise*. In

The Theory of the Leisure Class he had attempted to teach the Puritan people that they had not yet destroyed medieval barbarism; that they had not yet vanquished the dragon of chaos. In this book he wanted to reveal the weakness in seventeenth- and eighteenth-century Puritanism which had made it so difficult to define the existence of the dragon and had helped keep the Puritans at the mercy of the profane forces of evil.

To liberate themselves from the parasitical control of the feudal aristocracy, the early Puritans had developed a theory of private property as a "Natural Right." The great spokesman for the Puritan revolution, Locke, had appealed to a sacred state of nature against the profane civilization of medieval England. But Locke was wrong in assuming that in the state of nature, in the time of origin, private ownership existed. Locke and his followers could be sympathized with, Veblen declared, because they wanted to help men to be productive and constructive and they hoped to accomplish this by protecting the productive individual from the robber barons of the dark ages. And the system had not worked badly until the end of the eighteenth century because, up to that time, the property owned by most capitalists fulfilled Locke's description of private property as property with which a man had mixed his labor. This was the age of small artisans and merchants. This was an age of small producers.

By the beginning of the nineteenth century, however, individualistic capitalist production had given way to the mass production of the factory. The age of industrialism had begun, and Locke's definition no longer described this new economic situation. The men who worked in the factories did not own them, and they did not own the production of the factories, that with which they mixed their labor. In theory and in law individual capitalists owned the factories. But factory production, Veblen declared, depended upon the co-operation of the entire community. In fact, then, the factories belonged to all the people of the community. Productive property no longer made sense in the Lockean individualistic description. This was the terrible irony of the situation. Puritans attempting to escape from the parasitical medieval aristocracy had created a new parasitical class—that of finance capitalism.

The seventeenth- and eighteenth-century Puritans had been able to make the machine the dominant force in economic life, but the finance capitalists were in a strategic position to sabotage the machine because of the Lockean definition of private property. Englishmen had placed private property within the protection of impersonal law to protect it from the barbaric feudal lords whose values were honorific gains in meaningless warfare. And they had placed the government under the power of the businessman, apparently within the rational authority of a constitution, which supposedly guaranteed rule by objective law rather than personal whim. From within this institutional framework of artificial rational objectivity, they had created the process of machine production, the very essence of real rational objectivity.

The machine meant standardization of the economy and, ultimately, the whole of life. It was the logic of the machine to destroy human whim and to replace it with rational discipline and order. It was the logic of the machine to produce goods as economically as possible and to distribute them as efficiently as possible. All men were equal before the machine, and all must work efficiently, with certainty and expedition, to keep the machine process working with the regularity of clockwork. This was the final definition of the influence of the machine of human life—that it forced all men to keep pace with the machine's ability to produce and distribute with the regularity of a clock. The machine demanded that men become as rational as the machine, and there had come to "prevail a degree of standardization and precise mechanical adjustment of the details of everyday life, which presumes a facile and unbroken working of all those processes that minister to these standardized human wants." [18]

The factories, however, were technically owned by the finance capitalists, and these men lived in an unreal, irrational, artificial world. Their values were still the predatory ones of the feudal past expressed as a desire for profits and not production. Their economic world was the world of paper money and abstract credit which had no functional relationship to the concrete facts of productive wealth. And they made their profits by sabotaging the productive economy to create fluctuations in this artificial money market which worked to their personal gain. These raids, then, were comparable to the honorific gains of feudal barons. These modern robber barons were men of whim. They still lived in the profane time and space of barbaric civilization; they lived in a man-made social environment dominated by human values. In every way possible Veblen stressed that there was no concrete reality in this world of the finance capitalist. Puritanical capitalism had regressed into medieval darkness.

These finance capitalists were much more dangerous dragons than the decadent leisure class described in his first book. They posed a direct threat to the harmony of the machine and the factory. And they knew how to use the continued commitment of the Puritan people to private property as natural and sacred to protect and further their disruptive schemes. Once again, however, Veblen promised his people that the force of light, the force of the machine process, would overcome the force of darkness, the force of the parasitical aristocracy. Once again, he pointed out that the robber barons had the power only of man-made institutions and traditions, power that was necessarily ephemeral. Once again he pointed out that the machine process was "an irruption of the sacred into the world," repeating the paradigm of the time of origin, repeating that original reality which "neither changes nor is it exhausted." The seventeenth- and eighteenth-century Puritans had not created the machine process in the sense that it was artificial, the product of human imagination. They had only rediscovered and repeated the paradigm of productivity which had characterized the timeless and harmonious world of prehistoric savagery. Again the clash between the leisure class and the producer class would be that of the ephemeral and profane and the eternal and sacred:

The ultimate ground of validity for the thinking of the business classes is the natural rights ground of property—a conventional, anthropomorphic fact having an institutional validity, rather than a matter-of-fact validity such as can be formulated in terms of material cause and effect; while the classes engaged in the machine industry are habitually occupied with matters of causal sequence, which do not level themselves to statement in anthropomorphic terms of natural rights and which afford no guidance in questions of institutional right and wrong, or of conventional reason and consequence.[19]

Veblen now described the factory with images which evoked the temple of primitive man where sacred space and sacred time were to be found in all their purity. The factory, organized for production, did repeat the paradigm of the time of origin when productivity was imposed upon chaos. The workers, coming into this sacred space, were able to escape the corrupting influence of the false values of the profane society in which they lived, and were transported back to the sacred time of origin. They became complete Puritans purged of all human and profane attitudes.

While finance capitalists, their lawyers and judges, tried to interpret "new facts in terms of accredited precedents, rather than a revision of the knowledge drawn from past experience in the matter-of-fact light of new phenomena," the machine had lifted the masses from bondage to tradition, and the legal structure of absolute property rights was being questioned by the juries who "speak for the untrained sympathies of the vulgar." [20] The masses no longer took their values from precedent but from the machine:

What the discipline of the machine industry inculcates, therefore, in the habits of life and of thought of the workman, is regularity of sequence and mechanical precision. . . . Mechanically speaking, the machine is not his to do with it as his fancy may suggest. His place is to take thought of the machine and its work in terms given him by the process that is going forward.[21]

The working majority involved in the productive work of the factories was leading the way, therefore, to a fresh adjustment of society to its economic basis. There was no way that finance capitalism could halt this trend, because its profits came from the productivity of the machine. If the finance capitalists destroyed the machine, society would revert back directly to the medieval past and the old feudal aristocracy would destroy the financiers. On the other hand, if the bankers continued to accept the machine, they must also accept their own rapid destruction because the machine was destroying the institution of private property. "Broadly, the machine discipline acts to disintegrate the institutional heritage of all degrees of antiquity and authenticity. . . . It thereby cuts away that ground of law and order on which business enterprise is founded." [22]

In this developing world of absolute objectivity all of mankind was on the road to salvation; it was escaping from a profane history in which men had been trapped between outmoded institutional values and institutional situations. The machine would guarantee that there would be no more ephemeral historical values because "mechanically employed classes, trained to matter-of-fact habits of thought, show a notable lack of spontaneity in the construction of new myths or conventions as well as in the reconstruction of the old." [23] With tongue in cheek, Veblen could share a joke with his Puritan audience when he wrote: "The machine is a leveler, a vulgarizer, whose end seems to be the extirpation of all that was respectable, noble and dignified in human intercourse and ideals." What he and his readers understood was that the machine was destroying predatory ideals, was destroying all of that tragic history of vicious barbarism which had kept men from living by the truly noble instincts which had characterized the sacred time of origin.

A third book, *The Instinct of Workmanship,* was now written to complete Veblen's grand scheme of outlining the tragic fall of man from the sacred time of origin into the profane time of barbarism and man's triumphant ritual of the eternal return to sacred time. He was ready to explain how modern industrialism and science was "a symbolic repetition of the cosmogony" which was reinstating man into the Eden of the past. And he was prepared to argue that man would never fall again. Veblen began by reconstructing in detail the ancient conditions that must have made men what they inherently were:

This savage mode of life, which was, and . . . is native to man, would be characterized by a considerable group solidarity within a relatively small group, living very near the soil, and unremittingly dependent for their daily life on the workmanlike efficiency of all the members of the group. The prime requisite for survival under these conditions would be a propensity unselfishly and impersonally to make the most of all the material means at hand and a penchant for turning all resources of knowledge and materials to account to sustain the life of the group.[24]

Veblen was teaching his final lesson to his fellow Puritans. They had prized productivity and hated parasites; they had prized peace and hated war; they had prized common sense and hated the artificial. But they had believed that these good traits were to be found in a retreat from medievalism to a state of nature characterized by private property held by the self-reliant individual. Now he was teaching them that there was no private property in the state of nature. There were natural rights, the natural instincts of primitive man that "alone make anything worthwhile," but they were the rights of the interdependent group, not the isolated individual. They were the rights of productive property held in common. There was the instinct of workmanship that led men to high social and material productivity and pride in the jobs; the instinct of parental bent which was broader than family feeling and led to a broad humanitarianism and concern for the welfare of the whole community; and the instinct of idle curiosity which is the basis of all matter-of-fact knowledge leading to scientific progress.

There was perfect harmony in the original creation, in the

sacred, timeless creation. But man fell and profane time began. Why? For Veblen the dragon of chaos was within man himself. In a sense man rebelled against the original creation because he used imagination. Out of his imagination man constructed the artificial structure of profane institutions and traditions that imprisoned him and thwarted his productive instincts which could have kept him in harmony with the real world. This was the fatal flaw in mankind—imagination.

The sacred temple of the machine, the factory, was now, however, providing the discipline which forced man to think only in matter-of-fact terms. Imagination was brought under control and repressed. The fruitful instincts were liberated, and man could live perpetually in harmony with the sacred time of origin because the machine would never allow imagination to create that false, artificial, and profane world of timeful history again. Man, under the discipline of the machine, would engage in the eternal repetition of the paradigmatic gestures. Never again would men engage in the "vain and illusory activity" that had sprung from "their own initiative."

Writing in 1910 after two decades of muckraking that had reported the continued presence of medieval barbarism in the United States and western Europe, Veblen was prepared to prophesy that profane patterns of culture were soon to disappear and the moment of ultimate restoration to the sacred time of origin was at hand. His article, "Christian Morals and the Competitive System," reveals how much he saw his prophecy as only the final fulfillment of that first Puritan prophecy of 1600. The Puritans of the seventeenth century had argued that the church of Rome, the church of medieval civilization, was the anti-Christ, the lair of the dragon of chaos. They had argued that before the creation of this human church, this man-made institution with its profane historical traditions, there had existed the true Christian church, God-given and not man-made, timeless and not timeful, sacred and not profane. Veblen now demonstrated his agreement that before there was the false, historical church, there had been an authentic, a real Christianity of the time of origin.

He began his essay by stating that modern civilization in 1900 seemed to be based on two major traditions, competitive capitalism and Christianity. And he asked: "Do they further and fortify one another? Do they work together without mutual help or hindrance? Or do they mutually inhibit and defeat each other?" These questions were important, Veblen stated, because they led to a still more basic question: Could modern civilization survive if one or the other of these traditions disappeared?

The answers to all the questions were to be found only through an examination of the historical background of Christianity and capitalism. True Christianity, original, natural, noninstitutional, and nontraditional, was based on two principles: humility and brotherly love. It appeared as a force in Western civilization during the collapse of the Roman Empire for two reasons which illuminate the two principles that were its spiritual foundation. In the first instance, that of humility, the discipline of daily life for most people was the experience of defeat and the necessity of submission. This, then, was the cultural source of humility in the habits of a disintegrating empire. Brotherly love, however, came not from habit but from the destruction of habit. During this period of social disaster, "The pride of caste and all the principles of differential dignity and honor fell away, and left mankind naked and unashamed and free to follow the promptings of hereditary savage human nature which make for fellowship and Christian charity." [25] This, to Veblen, explained the lasting power of Christianity through the ages. It was based on an eternal human nature which "springs eternal" when the pressure of conventionality is removed. There is a timeless Christianity which expressed the sacred time of origin.

As against this eternal and immutable bedrock on which Christianity was grounded, Veblen stated that the competitive traditions of finance capitalism went back no farther than the "eighteenth century and reflected the cultural values of this limited historical period." Anchored only on ephemeral habits of mind and the institutions that rested on those habits, the profane competitive principle was disappearing from a world in which the machine process was inculcating new habits of thought.

Veblen was now in a position to answer his questions concerning the relations of true Christianity and the competitive system. They did not further each other, they did not help each other, nor did they mutually defeat one another. One was growing stronger, and one was dying. One represented the immutably sacred values of harmonious human nature, the other was a timeful and profane moment of an artificial society. Modern civilization must gain in stability by the disappearance of predatory capitalism. And the machine process not only guaranteed the destruction of this fragile tradition but it also was reinforcing the primitive instincts of workmanship, parental bent, and idle curiosity which were so much a part of natural Christianity. In his stilted and involuted prose, Veblen announced the coming recovery of the sacred time of origin:

There is little in the current situation to keep the natural right of pecuniary discretion in touch with the impulsive bias of brotherly love, and there is in the spiritual discipline much that makes for an effective discrepancy between the two. Except for a possible reversion to a cultural situation strongly characterized by ideals of emulation and status, the ancient racial bias embodied in the Christian principle of brotherhood should logically continue to gain ground at the expense of the pecuniary morals of competitive business.[26]

When World War I began in 1914 Veblen was ready to interpret this tragic event as a necessary moment of suffering which would speed the coming of the millennium, when the sacred time of origin would be restored. His book, *Imperial Germany and the Industrial Revolution,* applied his theological formulas to that unhappy nation. His readers had already learned that industrialism had appeared first in England because that nation was less burdened by medieval civilization than its continental neighbors. Englishmen, therefore, had remained closer to their original primitive natures and were attuned to this new economic system which repeated the peaceful and productive principles of the savage Eden.

Germany, or the multiplicity of petty German feudal states, was in direct contrast to England. More than almost any European group, the Germans had remained the prisoners of almost pure medievalism into the nineteenth century. Veblen hastened to stress that racially the Germans were no different from Englishmen or any other Europeans. He reassured his readers that biologically the mass of Germans were genetically linked to the innate peacefulness of prehistoric man. It was not the German people who had chosen war but their feudal lords.

Again Veblen emphasized that it was because of the primitive productive instincts of savage prehistory that the German people had turned so enthusiastically to industrialism when it crossed the channel from England in the nineteenth century. The fundamental biological impulse of the Germans which linked them to all of mankind was the impulse "of workmanship and fecundity rather than of dynastic power, statecraft, priestcraft, or artistic achievement." [27] Veblen's promise, therefore, was that the feudal war lords of Germany were unnatural, an artificial social aristocracy holding "irresponsible authority," and he reminded his readers that "The scheme of institutions in force in any given community . . . being of the nature of habit is necessarily unstable . . . whereas the type of any given racial stock is stable." [28] Warlike and profane Germany was ephemeral. Peaceful and sacred Germany was timeless and immutable.

It was Prussia, the most feudal and the least industrial of all the German states, which had dominated the unification of the nation and had set the national policy of an aggressive, predatory imperialism that had forced Europe into war in 1914. The violent, selfish, brutal aristocrats who controlled the government and the army were attempting to destroy the peaceful, productive English commonwealth and the progressive force of industrialism which was spreading from England to undermine feudalism throughout the entire world. This war, for Veblen, could be described as Armageddon, the final struggle of the forces of darkness and the forces of light. Imperial Germany was the last great stronghold of the medieval dragon of chaos. England was the cathedral from which the gospel of the sacred space and time of eternal harmony was radiating throughout all the nations to restore them to their original purity. And there was no way for the parasitical war lords of Imperial Germany to win this struggle because, to achieve the military might to defeat England, they had been forced to create a modern army built upon the productivity of industrialism. "The Imperial State [is] unable to get along without the machine industry, and, also, in the long run, unable to get along with it; since this industrial system in the long run undermines the foundations of the State." [29]

Once more, then, Veblen prophesied that the sacred, immutable, and eternal nature of the machine would defeat the profane, ephemeral traditions and institutions of a transitory historical society. He also had a final ironic bit of good news. It would be the German officer corps which would suffer the greatest casualties. Their death would immediately eliminate the evil aristocracy who imprisoned the good German people. The war would speed the inevitable victory of industrialism over feudalism.

By 1919 Veblen had been preaching the coming millennium for almost thirty years. For three decades he had promised that the force of industrialism, of the machine discipline, would easily sweep away every historical institution and tradition, all vestiges of profane time, and allow mankind once more to dwell by the eternal precepts of the harmonious time of origin. Throughout his messages of hope, which had spanned more than a generation, his optimism had focused on the mass of men, those most disciplined by the machine, those most purified by industrialism. In Veblen's Puritanism each man was to be a priest. But by 1919 Veblen's hopes for

an immediate millennium were seriously undermined. Imperial Germany was defeated, but this Armageddon had not
produced the victory of the forces of light. England and the
United States, the two most industrial nations, had emerged
victorious, but both continued to be ruled by a parasitical
aristocracy. What had gone wrong?

Reluctantly, Veblen admitted that the common man had
not seen the true light in the temple that was the factory.
The lies and deceits which the ruling capitalist class spread
through the press, the pulpit, the classrooms of the established order still so clouded the minds of the people that they
were unable to live by the discipline of the machine. They
could not, therefore, regain harmony with their inner biological nature of peace and productivity. They remained the
slaves of their external culturally imposed personalities which
encouraged them to conspicuous consumption and waste and,
even worse, encouraged them to admire the predatory values
of national war.

Between 1917 and 1919 Veblen had discovered that the financial capitalists of England and the United States were just
as committed to aggressive imperialism as the feudal aristocracy of Germany. And he had discovered that they had so
poisoned the mind of the common man through their manipulation of education that the people were seduced by the
false glory of the suicidal adventure of world war. If, by 1919,
Veblen could no longer predict that the masses passing
through the sacred space of the factory must necessarily have
their vision of a sacred time of origin restored, could he offer
any hope for victory over the dragon of chaos? Veblen
snatched at one more sign of salvation. He announced the
existence of a group of priests within the sacred spaces of the

industrial order—the engineers who served the machines.

Revising his description of the impact of industrialism, Veblen wrote:

It is only during the later decades of the modern era . . . that this mechanistic conception of things has begun seriously to affect the current system of knowledge and belief; and it has not hitherto seriously taken effect except in technology and in the material sciences so that it has not hitherto seriously invaded the established scheme of institutional arrangements, the system of law and custom. . . . the vested rights of absentee ownership are still embedded in the sentiments of the underlying population.[30]

The common man, the worker, was no longer the hope of the future. Only the actual operators of the factories, the engineers, were "soberly trained in a spirit of tangible performance and endowed with something more than an even share of the sense of workmanship." [31]

If the United States, if the industrialized nations, were to be saved from chaos, only the engineers had the spiritual and material ability to accomplish the preservation of the natural peaceful and productive harmony which was the underlying reality of all modern nations: "It is eminently a system, self-balanced and comprehensive; and it is a system of interlocking, mechanical processes rather than skillfull manipulation." [32] This marvelous, autonomous, economic structure which repreats the paradigm of the peaceful productivity of the time of origin will function in eternal harmony if its priests, the engineers, will protect it from the dragon of chaos symbolized by the finance capitalists.

Already the vested interests are again tightening their hold and are busily arranging for a return to business as usual; which means working at cross-purposes as usual, waste of work and materials as usual, restriction of output as usual, waste of superfluities as usual.

. . . a regime of continued and increasing shame and confusion, hardship and dissension, unemployment and privation, waste and insecurity of person and property.[33]

How long, how long, Veblen cried out in 1919, could the engineers, the holy men of industrialism, allow the sacred time of origin to be profaned by these evil, parasitical aristocrats? How long would it be before they accepted the responsibility that

The material welfare of all the advanced peoples rests in the hands of these technicians, if they will only see it that way, take counsel together, constitute themselves the self-directing General Staff of the country's industry, and dispense with the interference of the lieutenants of the absentee owners. Already they are strategically in a position to take the lead and impose their own terms of leadership, so soon as they . . . shall reach a common understanding to that effect and agree on a plan of action.[34]

Frantically, Veblen beseeched the engineers to recognize that they would not be engaging in a revolution by overthrowing the finance capitalists. The reality, the sacred reality of America, was industrialism, intrinsically self-balanced. The vested interests were not part of that system. They were alien to it. Their values were destructive of it. To destroy the absentee owners would destroy nothing real. This kind of revolution would be a conservation. "It would all of it neither subvert nor derange any substantial mechanical contrivance or relation, nor need it materially disturb the relations . . . of persons now engaged in productive industry. In fact the disallowance will touch nothing more substantial than a legal make-believe." [35] The engineers would not be guilty of violating the paradigmatic model of the time of origin by leading a revolution that swept away "what men do on their own initiative . . . without a mythical model." They would only purify the world of "vain and illusory activity."

Finally, Veblen's Puritan jeremiad prophesied doom if the engineers did not accept their religious responsibility to defend the harmony of the sacred from the chaos of the profane. This was Armageddon once more, but now there was no vision of the inevitable victory of the forces of light which had informed Veblen's earlier prophecies. The forces of darkness were now in a strategic position to reduce the citadels of sacred space and time to the profanity of total chaos:

That extent and degree of paralysis from which the civilized world's industry is suffering just now . . . goes to argue that the date may not be far distant when the interlocking processes of the industrial system shall have become so closely interdependent and so delicately balanced that even the ordinary modicum of sabotage involved in the conduct of business will bring the whole to a fatal collapse.[36]

The implications of this warning were catastrophic. Industrialism had been a second irruption of reality which had the power to bring mankind once more into organic unity with the primitive sacred time of origin. If industrialism, however, instead of finance capitalism, were now to be destroyed, mankind would probably wander forever in the meaningless and terrifying world of profane time. This, indeed, was Armageddon. Viewed from the perspective of Veblen's values, it would appear that his fears have been fulfilled; that we have lost our last opportunity to return to a sacred time of origin and that we have begun a perilous pilgrimage into the unpredictable future of profane history from which there is no turning back.

Background of Veblen's Thought

Joseph Dorfman

MORE THAN A DECADE AGO, in 1957, the American Economic Association celebrated the centennial of Thorstein Veblen's birth. I intended my address on that occasion as a valedictory on that now recognized seminal mind. The invitation to participate in a seminar on one of the greatest sons of Carleton College in connection with the celebration of her own centennial was, however, an honor and an obligation that could not be declined. In accepting the invitation I also thought that I might in this small way pay tribute to Veblen's first teacher in economics, John Bates Clark, who at Carleton laid the foundation for his fundamental contributions to the field. Indeed it may be reasonably argued that this then small, struggling frontier college produced two minds that perhaps had most to do with the shape of economic thinking in the United States in the first half of the twentieth century. Clark was to become the leading voice of the dominant marginalist approach to economic analysis, and Veblen was to become the chief source of the revisionist movement. Between them there always existed the admiration that the instructor has for the favorite pupil who has amply fulfilled his promise, and the student has for the sophisticated, disciplined teacher who has encouraged him to push forward the frontiers of knowledge.

This was not the first time that Carleton College had honored the memory of Veblen. There was another simpler but no less impressive commemoration over thirty-five years ago which perhaps some of the older members of the faculty may recall. Shortly after Veblen died in August, 1929, the *Carleton Circle* proclaimed that "taken as a whole there can be no doubt that his writings were more significant and more widely read than those of any other Carleton man." This may have been a rash statement at the time, for the country was at the height of a booming prosperity which most economists considered permanent. There seemed to be no serious national or international problems. Even some of Veblen's ablest students felt his work was in large part outmoded, and Veblen himself was aware of the lack of interest. The matter came up in 1928, in connection with the desire of a sister-in-law to obtain information from other members of the family for his biography. Veblen wrote his older brother Andrew [1] that he had little concern about her project, partly because "there is no probability of her getting anything printed. Possibly she might have got into print about me a few years ago; but that is all past now and I have gone off the program of news." [2]

Veblen's star, however, was not long in eclipse. The era after his death saw the Great Depression, the rise to power of Adolf Hitler and Fascism, World War II, the ascendancy of the Soviet and Communist China in world politics. Finally, and possibly most important of all, it saw the tremendous proliferation of technological advance, particularly in such areas as the harnessing of the atom, the entry into space, automation, and the development of the computer. With these events, Veblen's forecasts and insights, rather than

being outmoded, seemed strikingly modern. Certainly there
can no longer be any question of the enduring significance of
his work. It must be admitted that time, the basic test of the
importance of a thinker, has more than vindicated *The
Carleton Circle* and stamped this powerful philosopher of industrialism as a landmark, not only in the advance of knowledge in his discipline but also in the development of American civilization.

It was here at Carleton College that Veblen first manifested
and developed the extraordinary variety of interests—philosophy, psychology, biology, anthropology (including archeol-
ogy), cultural history, sociology, and economics—that he
would fuse in unusual ways into his comprehensive systematic
studies of the growth, functioning, and future of the current
economic and social order.

Carleton's role is intimately tied up with its place as a cita-
del of New England culture in the West. This "Yankee"
culture was one of the most powerful elements in the formation and growth of American civilization. Carleton was one of
a string of sturdy colleges that the sons of New England set
up in the West to inculcate the sound principles of Congrega-
tionalist—or, more properly, Puritan—New England. Transported also was the religious atmosphere of New England.
Students were expected to observe the strict Puritan order of
morals and to behave in conventional ways. The dominant
theme of the textbooks in what is now called the social sciences was a conception of human nature that saw man
motivated by self-interest, but with excesses restrained by the
powerful precepts of religion. In this view the role of the
state was limited to little more than enforcing contracts and
maintaining law and order against threat of foreign invasion

and domestic turbulence. Stated more urbanely, Carleton stood as did practically every college in the country for the "genteel tradition," as Veblen's greatest student, Wesley C. Mitchell put it. Of course this tradition put "conventional fetters upon free thought that bound most sons of New England" in Veblen's generation, "and bound none more tightly than the New Englanders born in the Middle West." [3]

To be sure, those blessed with an undue amount of idle curiosity, or "intellectual initiative" as Veblen described it, were able to a greater or lesser degree to emancipate themselves "by sheer dint of straight thinking, from the conventional fetters" and become leaders in the advance of knowledge. For Veblen, the process of emancipation was facilitated by his being an "outsider," that is, a rural Norwegian who had barely escaped being an immigrant. It was accelerated by Clark's sympathy and protection of "this particular student, whose unconventional character had not endeared him to the authorities of an institution where smoking was ground for expulsion and the professor of mathematics opened every class exercise with prayer." [4]

Clark, with his strong interest in ethical aspects of economic problems, was engaged in modernizing what he called the "antique orthodoxy" of the dominant classical economics into what came to be called "marginal utility theory." As previously noted, this would become the reigning orthodoxy by the time Veblen launched his own work, but in his youth it was somewhat controversial. So well apparently did he absorb this brand of "new economics" that, as the story goes, it was he who called Clark's attention to a similar but earlier work, *The Theory of Political Economy* (1871), by the British writer W. Stanley Jevons, who had spearheaded the movement in the Anglo-American world. Finding Veblen, as he stated later, "a man with a natural leaning toward the kind of work that requires exactness of thought and statement and extensive and careful research," Clark expected that he would become a "successful investigator, especially in philosophy and political economy." Clark encouraged Veblen to go on to graduate work at Johns Hopkins in 1881. He stayed barely a semester, but he found it invigorating. He took a course in history with Clark's friend and Amherst classmate, Herbert Baxter Adams, a pioneer in the introduction of German methods of research. In his major, philosophy, Veblen studied logic under Charles S. Peirce, the founder of pragmatism. He was so deeply impressed with George S. Morris, the teacher of John Dewey and one of the advance guard of trained Hegellians, that he took all three of his courses, including one on Kant's *The Critique of Pure Reason*.

In his minor subject, economics, he had as his teacher Richard T. Ely, who was fresh from German training and who would soon become the *enfant terrible* of the discipline. Veblen became increasingly interested in economics and for a while he thought of shifting his major to that subject. For the local club of students and faculty in the social sciences, The Historical and Political Science Association, he prepared a paper on "J. S. Mill's Theory of the Taxation of Land." Ely encouraged him to develop the address for publication in a journal, under the title of "The Relation of Rent to the Advance of Population," a topic which Veblen called "a vexed question." But, as he put it, the journal "died of it." [5] This experience, coupled with his failure to secure a scholarship at Johns Hopkins, led him to Yale without any change of his major.

At Yale a sharp controversy was going on between Veblen's teacher in philosophy, President Noah Porter, and his teacher in economics, William Graham Sumner of *The Folkways*, over the British writer Herbert Spencer's revolutionary application of the theory of evolution to philosophy and the social sciences. Porter stood for the traditional common sense philosophy and fought hard against the inroads of what he considered the atheism or agnosticism of Spencer's doctrine and the "disintegrating" idealist or "metaphysical" systems of Kant and Hegel.

Here, as throughout his career, Veblen's independence of mind manifested itself so that, despite their almost diametrically opposing views, he was able to appreciate both Porter and Sumner.[6] And once again, as in the case of J. B. Clark, we find Veblen receiving approval and help from these two men of essentially conservative social views. Both his teachers wrote letters of high praise recommending Veblen for teaching posts.

Despite the recommendations, Veblen, after receiving his doctorate in 1884, failed to obtain a college appointment. This was an era in which appointments to academic posts in the field of philosophy went primarily to holders of divinity degrees. Veblen, however, not only lacked this qualification but indeed was suspected of being an agnostic. As a further handicap, he had his status as an outlander, a "Norskie," a member of a minority then generally held in low esteem.

He spent the next seven years reading and thinking, first on his father's farm at Nerstrand and then, after his marriage in 1888 to his Carleton classmate Ellen Rolfe, at her father's farm at Stacyville, Iowa.[7] At the end of this period Andrew Veblen called a conference of the Veblen clan where it was

decided that the best way for Thorstein to overcome the
handicap of satisfactorily explaining an inactive period of
seven years was to begin again as a graduate student, but this
time in the social sciences. Accordingly, in the winter term of
1891, he entered Cornell University. There he attracted the
attention of the head of the department of economics, J.
Laurence Laughlin. Laughlin was probably the most traditional economist of the day. For him the marginalist theories
were pure nonsense, and he knew little and cared less for
Marx. Yet once again we find a staunchly orthodox teacher
attracted, as J. M. Clark put it, by Veblen's "intellectual
vitality and fund of wide and curious learning." [8] Soon after
Veblen came to his notice, Laughlin obtained for him a special grant from the authorities to enable him to continue at
Cornell. In 1892, when Laughlin became head of the department of the new University of Chicago, he took Veblen along
with him as a teaching fellow. There Veblen remained for
fourteen years, reaching the rank of assistant professor and at
the same time serving as managing editor of the *Journal of
Political Economy,* which Laughlin had established. At Chicago Veblen did his basic work, notably *The Theory of the
Leisure Class* (1899), *The Theory of Business Enterprise*
(1904), and the famous series of methodological essays in
1898–1901. These began with "Why is Economics Not an
Evolutionary Science?," continued with three on "The Preconceptions of Economic Science," and ended with "Industrial and Pecuniary Employments," better described by the
title he preferred, "The Distinction between Industrial and
Pecuniary Activity." [9]

In 1906, thanks largely to the efforts of the eminent zoolo-
gist, Jacques Loeb, he went to Stanford as an associate profes-

sor. This connection was dissolved after three years. In 1911, sponsored by still another friend of conservative social views, Herbert Joseph Davenport, he went to the University of Missouri, where he stayed six years as a "professorial lecturer." Here he published the last of his major works, *The Instinct of Workmanship and the State of the Industrial Arts* (1914), *Imperial Germany and the Industrial Revolution* (1915), and *An Inquiry into the Nature of Peace and the Terms of Its Perpetuation* (1917). After about one year each with the United States Food Administration, and the liberal weekly, *The Dial*, he began in 1919 to lecture at the recently established New School for Social Research in New York. These lectures were discontinued by 1925, in part for lack of funds and in part because Veblen felt that he lacked the energy to continue teaching. In 1926 he went into "cold storage" and died three years later on the eve of the Great Depression.

The many changes of posts, generally involuntary, indicate that Veblen was an irritant, both intellectually and personally, to the Establishment of his day; but if he had been no more than this, he would long since have been forgotten. The real importance of his career lies in his penetrating insights into the fundamental workings of western society. While not an exponent of specific reforms, he served as a catalyst. In his theories, active reformers found a rationale and stimulus.

Veblen came on the scene when America was changing from a primarily rural, agricultural society to an urban, highly industrialized society. The change brought with it both the promise of material advance heretofore undreamed of and a host of vexing social problems. In turn the advance of urbanization and industrialization forced the intellectual community (particularly that portion of it which we generally categorize as liberal) to re-examine the social and economic philosophy that had dominated the whole era between the founding of the nation and the Civil War. *Laissez faire* had been the cornerstone of the dominant egalitarian Jefferson-Jackson idealogy; so much had laissez faire become a term of commendation that the ardent believers in heavy protective tariffs struggled to define the tariff to make its theorists the only true exponents of laissez faire.

The spokesmen for laissez faire had sharply criticized the special privileges and prerequisites of the aristocratic class which they maintained enriched a few idlers at the expense of the industrious mass of the people. To them the privileges established by law were the source of hated monopoly and resulted in the impoverishment of the vast majority, accompanied by social turbulence and even the threat of the destruction of the republican form of government. The principle of free competition was conceived as the application of self-assertion to man's economic activity. Thus Thomas Jefferson, as he sought to eliminate the holdovers of political feudalism, could be an admirer of Adam Smith's *The Wealth of Nations* and its demand for "the simple and obvious system of natural liberty;" and Andrew Jackson and his followers, as they laid the foundations of the tradition of free enterprise, could advocate and bring about the passage of measures which conformed to the doctrines of David Ricardo.

But as the nation underwent rapid industrialization during the 1870s and 1880s, the astonishing material advances were accompanied by a host of economic and social problems. For the first time the nation witnessed large, violent clashes between the wage-earning and the new capitalist-owner classes. The extension of the railroads westward combined with radical technological advances in agriculture largely brought an end to the relatively self-sufficient rural economy which Veblen had known as a youth. The average farmer who heretofore had minimal contact with the institutions of a modern money economy soon found himself caught up in the complexities of dealing with banks and other money lenders, millers, grain elevators, commodity exchanges, and freight rate structures. Because of his unfamiliarity with accounts and figures and legal technicalities, the uneducated and especially the immigrant farmer was at a disadvantage in dealing even with honest businessmen. And unfortunately all too often he became an easy target for those who charged usurious interest rates and discriminatory and excessive freight and elevator rates and for unscrupulous grain dealers. These burdens, added to the normal risks of weather, crop failures, and price fluctuations, built up the resentments which led to the succession of agrarian crusades. With the increasing concentration of population in cities came the ills of overcrowded slums, the criminal mobs, and the corrupt political machines.

The early fortunes in the nation were derived primarily from land, commerce, and banking; now the industrial expansion produced a whole new class of rich men who soon eclipsed the older ones, not only in the magnitude of their fortunes but even more spectacularly in the magnitude of their personal expenditures. These new magnates built gaudy palaces to display their success and also to serve as proof of financial solvency. The established legal arrangements seemed to provide no effective means for coping with the unbridled, piratical activities of those in control of the industrial, railroad, and financial empires.

Another source of discontent was the disorderly disposal of the vast western public lands. With the greater complexity and interdependence of the economy, such problems as money panics and depressions seemed to become much more chronic, of greater duration, and carried in their wake much suffering. The founders of the Jefferson-Jackson liberalism had never envisioned the kind of institutions which grew up with new technology. Thus the very laissez faire policies which they had advocated to free the mass of people from enslavement of the old mercantilist doctrine resulted to a large extent in the very things that they feared.

The economists who enjoyed the highest prestige in the immediate post Civil War era, led by Sumner, Laughlin, and the writers in the influential *Nation,* recognized the existence of these problems, but they generally took the view that the present competitive or laissez faire system was as satisfactory as possible under the circumstances. They contended that the ills either resulted from defects of human nature (and were therefore ineradicable), or they were the transient effects of economic development, or the consequences of unwise state interference such as protective tariffs, or of ignorant agitation to tamper with the gold standard, or of the importation of subversive revolutionary ideas from the European continent, especially central and eastern Europe. They believed in an oversimplified, mechanical doctrine of wages which held that the rate of wages was determined by natural economic law; therefore any attempt to set wages by other means such as collective bargaining or minimum wage legislation would result in damage to society in reduced employment and production. Thus the most popular textbook reduced the determination of wages to a matter of simple, arithmetical division. The part of capital that goes for the payment of wages is the dividend; the number of laborers is the divisor. Therefore "the quotient will be the general average rate of wages at that time and place. This principle invariably determines the current rate of wages in any country." [10]

Depressions were viewed as "natural tides in business" and not entirely unhealthy because they seemed to eliminate inefficient businessmen. There was agreement on the possibility of remediably reducing the severity of these "commercial crises," as they were called, by monetary and banking reform that would eliminate money panics. There was no agreement, however, on specific measures. On this question, as well as any other involving more than the most limited government intervention, the orthodox economists were guided by the ethical thesis that government action was inevitably an arbitrary, despotic force from the outside that would not achieve the necessary internal change in personal character. Into the orthodox position on specific policies, however, there was creeping a view that had been more common in Europe, namely, that the expansion of luxury was a powerful incentive or enticement to the increase of production and industrial advance, and that a wealthy leisure class offered the means of developing higher standards of taste, culture, and the like.

The vast majority of academic economists held the view that the main principles of the science had already been laid down clearly in the works of Adam Smith, Malthus, and Ricardo and that the tasks remaining were largely those of extension, interpretation, and refinements. However, vigorous intellectual controversy was stirring in other disciplines, and within a decade or so these controversies spilled over into economics. So fundamental was the impact that the consensus within the profession was destroyed and has not reappeared since.

At the vortex of the intellectual ferment were the ideas stemming from the Darwinian theory of evolution. The outstanding philosophical exponent of applying evolutionary doctrine, as noted above, was Spencer. Veblen had his first contact with Spencer's work at Carleton College. Probably of particular interest to Veblen was Spencer's effort to demonstrate that the methods of investigation employed in the physical sciences could be applied to the study of social life. Veblen also found interesting the use of anthropological material to explain the development of social and economic institutions. Spencer viewed social evolution as a process of advance, but, like his American disciple Sumner, he held that evolution as the survival of the fittest necessitated "the defeat of the many" and the enormous waste of "life and the possibilities of life." [11] Thus he declared in the 1872 edition of *Social Statics* that "the poverty of the incapable, the distresses that come upon the imprudent, the starvation of the idle, and those shoulderings aside of the weak by the strong, which leave so many 'in the shallows and in miseries,' are the decrees of a large far-seeing benevolence." This conclusion was seized upon by the staunchest advocates of dominant, extreme laissez faire economics as buttressing their position.[12]

But shortly afterwards a different view of evolution began to grow increasingly popular, a view most clearly formulated by the dean of American sociologists, Lester Frank Ward, who was among the early admirers of Veblen's work. Ward acknowledged his indebtedness to Spencer, and like him viewed social evolution as the process of advance; but he went on to argue that natural selection had produced an intelligent being, man, capable of consciously modifying his environment. Answering the charge of laissez faire thinkers that such efforts on the part of man were artificial, contrary to natural law, and therefore disruptive to progress, he argued that since man and his intelligence were also a part of nature, the sharp distinction between artificial and natural was invalid.[13] Since these artificial decisions were actually a part of the course of natural selection, society's first duty, Ward explained, was to educate the mass so as to elevate and expand man's reasoning powers. For, he declared, "increase of wisdom can alone realize higher degrees of social development." [14] Veblen sympathized with Ward's position. To him evolution was simply an accurate description of a historical process but not a tool for drawing sharp distinctions between that which is natural and that which is unnatural or artificial.

This was the period, too, when anthropology, in which Veblen had already manifested a deep interest at Carleton College, was achieving status as a separate discipline, the science of the development of culture.[15] The great pioneers in the United States were Lewis H. Morgan and Franz Boas. Morgan argued, in the celebrated *Ancient Society* (1877), that contrary to current vulgarized economics the institution of private property was not instinctive. It came rather late in man's development and did not appear in its present form until man began living in civilized social communities. In more recent times the passion for ownership has produced a "greed philosophy" to the point where it has become an unmanageable power and, indeed, a threat to society itself. He hoped, along with Ward, that human intelligence would rise to "the mastery over property, and define the relations of the state to the property it protects, as well as the obligations and the limits of the rights of its owners. The interests of society are paramount to individual interests and the two must be brought into just and harmonious relations."

Veblen found the ideas of Boas, of contemporary anthropologists, most attuned to his own. In the famous study of the primitive Kwakiutl Indians of British Columbia, Boas pointedly noted that the institution of private property gave rise to what Veblen, who was familiar with the work, later described as conspicuous waste. According to Boas, the method of obtaining rank and distributing property among these primitive Indians was by means of the potlach, whose operating principle was the interest-bearing investment of property. The recipient of such a distribution at a gift feast would not refuse the "gift" although it was actually a loan which must be repaid (refunded) with a hundred percent interest. The possession of wealth was honorable, and each Indian vigorously endeavored to acquire a fortune in order to outdo a rival by means of a potlach. Boas also noted that in an earlier period of the tribe's history "feats of bravery counted as well as distributions of property, but nowadays, as the Indians say, 'rivals fight with property only.' " He remarked that the potlach has a counterpart in modern civilized society in ostentatious expenditure of money to demonstrate superiority over detested rivals. In a preliminary report he commented, as would Veblen later, that the institution was "founded on psychical causes as active in our civilized society as among the barbarous natives of British Columbia." [16] Such evidence from primitive societies became the basis of Veblen's criticism of the "economic man" psychology employed by neoclassical economics, particularly marginal utility theory.

In the field of philosophy the period saw a decline, although not without a struggle, of the relatively naïve, Calvinistic, Scottish, Common Sense philosophy which had been dominant in the United States for over a hundred years. This had been the mainstay of Veblen's intellectual diet at Carleton and had been vigorously defended at Yale by president Porter. Its advocates appealed to the "common sense of mankind" for the ultimate validation of fundamental truths such as the existence of God and the urge of private property. By the time Veblen returned to academic halls in the 1890s, philosophical speculation in America was coming increasingly under the influence of the idealist philosophy of Kant and Hegel. It was these two conflicting streams—the idealist on the one hand, and the common sense on the other—which spawned that most peculiarly American philosophical school we now call pragmatism. Parallel to and strongly bound up with the growth of pragmatism was "functional" psychology.

The first extensive statement of pragmatism came from Veblen's teacher, C. S. Peirce, in the 1870s. Peirce's fellow spirit, William James, is generally credited with being the originator of functional psychology. A decade or so later, John Dewey, of whom Veblen was a colleague at the University of Chicago, developed and expanded the thoughts of Peirce and James to the point where pragmatism became (and still is) the dominant philosophy of America. The outgrowth of functional psychology created a revolution in American education. Dewey insisted the "the mental life must be stated in active terms, those of impulse and its development" and not in the "passive terms of mere feelings of pleasure and pain." [17] In short, from this evolutionary standpoint of the development of action what people saw, heard, felt, tasted, or smelled depended on what they were doing.

"In our purposively organized life we inevitably come back
upon previous conduct as the determining condition of what
we sense at any one moment, and the so-called external
stimulus is the occasion, and not the cause for this." [18] Although the backgrounds and modes of presentation of Dewey
and Veblen were very different, there is a striking, indeed
almost startling, similarity in their criticisms of the hedonist
philosophy and their employment of functional psychology
toward the understanding of economic behavior.

In the realm of economics, classical doctrine, as previously
noted, despite its overwhelming dominance within professional ranks, was being increasingly questioned from without
the profession. The problems produced by the industrial
revolution in the United States had reached proportions
where they could no longer be ignored, even by some of the
nation's staunchly conservative elements. A trustees' committee of Columbia University (hardly a radical group) complained in 1877 that the dominant economics was of little
help "in regard to matters which concern the very fountain
springs of national prosperity." The wide differences among
supposed expert solutions to current problems meant that
"either the truth of the assumed general principles of the
theoretic writers is denied, or it is claimed that their principles are only true with so many qualifications and limitations
that they were useless." [19]

Perhaps even more important in its influence on the nation's thinking was the arrival on the scene for the first time
of a highly popular radical literature. By far the best known
was Henry George's *Progress and Poverty* (1879) and Edward
Bellamy's *Looking Backward* (1888). Essentially George argued that the rental value of land did not derive from the

effort of an individual but rather was a product of society. To eliminate poverty and depressions, therefore, the state should levy a 100 per cent tax on this "unearned increment." Bellamy felt that the competitive, acquisitive extremes of capitalism ran contrary to Christian ethics and threatened the destruction of civilized society. He advocated an utopian socialist scheme. Veblen had read *Progress and Poverty* while at Carleton College and he and his wife read *Looking Backward* aloud in his retreat. According to his wife, shortly after this reading he decided definitely to make economics his area of study. We do not know what particularly impressed Veblen about the book, but it may well have been the emphasis on the abundance that modern machine technology made possible, and the wastes of resources under the existing relatively unrestrained system of business enterprise. The wastes ranged from severe business depressions to competitive, ostentatious living.

The first real challenge to classical economics within the profession came from the German historical school, which became prominent after the Civil War. A number of America's ablest young economists learned of this school first hand while studying in Germany in the post Civil War period. They heard penetrating criticism of the rigid restrictions and narrowness of British classical economic thought, accompanied by persuasive appeals for a much broader definition of the scope of the science of economics. At this time, in Europe as well as in the United States, the systematic collection and interpretation of historical and statistical data as we know it today had hardly begun. The historical school was among the first to recognize the tremendous possibilities of these methods as tools of investigation. The school also attempted to give greater scope to the ethical aspect of man and the relation of economics to the other social sciences, especially law, than classical economics would tolerate. They translated this thinking into practical terms for dealing with current social problems, in answer to Marxian socialism on the one hand and extreme laissez faire on the other. They offered perhaps the first comprehensive program for social security legislation, including sickness, workmen's compensation, old age, and unemployment. These proposals provided the basis for the actual measures which were enacted during Bismarck's regime.

The Americans who studied in Germany, while impressed with the work of the historical school, in particular the emphasis on greater use of statistical and empirical methods, for the most part returned to the United States still committed to classical doctrine. For a few, however, the experience sharply altered their thinking. Foremost among this group was Henry Carter Adams of the University of Michigan, the first statistician of the Interstate Commerce Commission. He transformed and adapted the work of the historical school to the American scene and its problems. On one important issue, however, he disagreed sharply with the school. This was their tendency to expand the conception of the State to include (practically) all society.[20] At the same time that he admired many of the reforms of Bismarck's welfare program, he criticized the use of the state to impose arbitrary and unnecessary restrictions on personal freedom. On much the same basis he opposed the fixing by government of wages and hours of labor. He admitted that the advent of large-scale industry had outdated the older idea of individual wage bargaining between the employee and his employer. In its place he envisioned a system of collective bargaining which was in effect a crystallization or codification of labor rights under common law and thus consonant with the Anglo-American concept of liberty.

On this, as well as on a whole range of social issues involving the role of the state, Adams sought to find a middle ground between the liberal tradition of almost completely unrestrained individualism envisioned by classical economics and the almost dictatorial state envisioned by the Germans. With an optimism which is so typical of much American thought, he believed it was possible to eradicate the major ills (for example, inhuman exploitation of workers) which had developed under industrial society, and at the same time to preserve and strengthen the essential advantages of competition and entrepreneurial freedom.

In the long run the chief effect of the historical school on the discipline of economics in the United States lay in the general acceptance of its view that statistical and historical data provided useful tools for dealing with current economic problems. This change of attitude is so complete that for us today it is difficult to conceive of operating a modern economy without the vast array of data available.

The period from the end of the Civil War to the close of the century was one of enormous industrial growth, but this expansion was by no means uniform. It was interrupted by several severe depressions of substantial duration which brought with them considerable unemployment and financial hardship. Orthodox doctrine, when not myopically overlooking depression, denied that such phenomena required either reshaping of existing doctrine or the adoption of strong corrective measures by the government. But in the eighties a number of economists, both orthodox and heterodox, began to question whether there might not be a strong causal relationship between the recurrent industrial depressions and the surges of overinvestment in heavy capital-goods industries. From this line of thinking, the overproduction-underconsumption theory associated with the name of the British heterodox economist John A. Hobson was developed, and this in turn became the basis of the permanent unemployment doctrine popularized by J. M. Keynes in the 1930s. Perhaps the most notable and influential of the orthodox economists to articulate the general overproduction doctrine was, somewhat unexpectedly, the extremely conservative David A. Wells. In *Recent Economic Changes* (1889) he suggested that constant improvements in technology made possible greater quantities of goods at lower prices. The individual industrialist in his desire to increase profits continued to expand capacity by additional capital investment. At the same time other producers pursued similar courses to the point where the amount of goods produced was greatly in excess of the demand that would take away the goods at profitable prices.[21] He also advanced the rather intriguing idea that the spectacular growth of demand for and trading in negotiable securities was another cause of overproduction. In effect he reversed the usual orthodox view that securities were floated as a means of raising funds for the creation of new and needed industry. Rather, industry was created without regard to need but only to satisfy the demand for securities.[22] Veblen, in one of his first articles on returning to the academic world in 1890, took over and developed portions of Wells's ideas.

No doubt, the thing that caught Veblen's attention in Wells's doctrine was an instance of a conservative, fundamentally orthodox economist introducing into his analysis (perhaps by the back door) the historical approach. Tacitly, Wells was admitting that current events could not be fully explained by the static analysis of classical economics but required the use of historical and statistical materials and the recognition of existing institutional patterns.

I have previously pointed out the oddity of Veblen's having been helped at several junctures of his career by men of highly conservative, orthodox views, views that indeed were practically opposite to his own. Let us here note a similar oddity in that Veblen's thinking apparently was deeply influenced by minds that were among the most conservative of their time, notably such men as Spencer, Sumner, Porter, and Wells. The answer to the why of this, I think, lies in large part in the fact that none of these men was so tied to static analysis that he overlooked the inherent dynamics of social institutions. Similarly, Veblen's sharpest criticisms of the economics profession were aimed at the dogmatic adherence to orthodox doctrine which was divorced from reality and which blocked understanding of social processes.

It seems to me that coming from without the power structure gives a special advantage to an interpreter of the social scene. The thinking of such individuals is less likely to be fettered by preconceptions which usually are inculcated in the members of the Establishment. And while this "Man from Mars" vantage point is helpful in understanding even a relatively static society, it is an especially valuable aid to insight in times of unusually rapid and far-reaching social and economic change, such as the period in which Veblen reached maturity. Indeed, it is reasonable to query whether the particular kind of original, fundamental speculations offered us by Veblen would have been possible had he sprung from the

main stream of our society. For example, would it have occurred to the hypothetical Man in the Mainstream to doubt
the hedonistic psychology of the economic man of classical
economics? Would those rare individuals who questioned
orthodox demand doctrine have had the daring to compare
the modern-day patterns of conspicuous consumption to the
emulative customs of the primitive Indian tribes of British
Columbia? But Veblen, free to follow his reasoning wherever
it led, was able to see demand as a complex, often illogical result of irrational, subconscious impulses and institutionally
induced, emulative desires.

Some of Veblen's most original insights were concerned
with such closely entwined modern capitalist institutions as
the money economy, the machine process, and the giant corporation. To point up how great was Veblen's departure
from the dominant thinking let us contrast his view of the
corporation with that of the Man in the Mainstream. Both
were agreed that in order to reap the benefits of modern technology, some form of organization was necessary to bring together large agglomerations of productive and financial
power under central control. But where the Man in the
Mainstream optimistically concluded that such concentrations
would naturally be translated into more goods at lower prices
(as envisioned by pure competition doctrine) Veblen saw the
giant corporation as inherently destructive of pure competition. To Veblen the corporation was no automatic neutral
mechanical device but a complex, many-sided institution
replete with multiple conflicts of interest, inefficiencies, and
wastes. These wastes and inefficiencies were not the fault of
the engineers and modern technologists, whose work he admired and at times seemed almost awed by. The fault lay

with those in control of corporations who were habituated to maintaining their power and maximizing their own pecuniary gains. As a result they were often engaged in financial manipulations which were detrimental to productive efficiency. The modern corporation was thus an instance of an important general principle of institutional behavior: namely, the institutions which man creates for his own benefit have a way of turning around, developing a life all their own, and threatening to become his masters and gods. No doubt this was the sort of thinking that one of Veblen's most eminent students was referring to when he said:

To a well brought up scion of American culture, taking one of Veblen's courses meant employing vivisection without an anaesthetic. Those who could stand the treatment, and not all could, came out with a much more critical attitude that included Veblen's own methods of arriving at conclusions—not at all a comfortable state of mind, but one that has marked advantages if one wishes to do scientific work.23

In closing I would like to say a little about the legacy of Veblen. To indicate the extent to which his thinking has permeated social and economic policy, let me again turn to the device of the Man in the Mainstream. With few exceptions, as we have seen, Veblen's contemporaries within the power structure were unable or did not dare to view society in his terms. Moreover, to the extent that his ideas were understood, they were viewed as dangerously radical. Yet today in one of those odd twists of history, we find the very epitome of modern Man in the Mainstream, that Leader of Consensus, President Johnson, in his messages to Congress in 1965 embracing Veblenian terminology and concepts. The waste of which Veblen spoke in *The Theory of the Leisure Class* comes to mind when the President speaks of the "presence of untapped productive capacity" and of the policies comprising

our . . . strategy of attack on waste. The waste of lives and property and progress which is the cost of war; the waste of human potential and self respect which is the cost of poverty and lack of opportunity; the waste of excessive government personnel, obsolete installations, and outmoded public services which is the cost of inefficient government; the waste of men and facilities and resources which is the cost of economic stagnation.

The President insisted further:

We do not intend to live in the midst of abundance, isolated from neighbors and nature, confined by blighted cities and bleak suburbs, stunted by a poverty of learning and an emptiness of leisure. The great society asks not how much but how good; not only how to create wealth but how to use it; not only how fast are we going but where we are headed.

Reflecting Veblen's emphasis on the never-ending industrial revolution, the President said that "ceaseless change" was the "hallmark of a progressive and dynamic economy." Even the language of the most technical of Veblen's critiques of orthodox economic thinking and its practical meaning, the famous "Preconceptions of Economic Science," is found in one of the President's basic conclusions: "Economic policy has begun to liberate itself from the preconceptions of an earlier day." [24]

Recollections of Veblen

Isador Lubin

In 1916 I came to the University of Missouri as a graduate student in sociology with a fellowship of 500 dollars. During my first semester I took a course with Veblen which he called Economic Factors in Civilization. There were a dozen of us in the class. Veblen sat on a small platform and talked in a low monotonous droning voice. He never had a note in front of him. He just talked for the fifty minutes and then asked if there were any questions. Usually there were none. I had the impression that there were no questions because very few of the students knew what he was talking about. But he did give us reading references. The thing that impressed me about the references was that many of them were Smithsonian Institution reports, and they had to do with the South Sea Islands. At first I could not figure out what that part of the world had to do with economic development. The fact was that he was really giving us a course which was a variant on *The Instinct of Workmanship,* and those of us who had read his book soon realized it. But few in the class had read the book, and consequently few understood what he was talking about. There were no examinations in the course, but there was a term paper.

One day I had difficulty in following his discussion, being

from a middle-sized city in Massachusetts, with virtually no knowledge of agriculture or the economics of agriculture. I took issue with something he said about agricultural economies. He looked at me and said "Lubin, it's very evident that you were brought up on the pavements." That closed the argument. Later I asked for an appointment so that I could clear up some ideas that I had and be sure I had understood what he had been saying. When I asked for the appointment he seemed delighted. It was my first personal contact with him, and I found him very cordial and friendly. It soon became evident that he had a respect for people who had curiosity and wanted to find out what things were about. It seemed that the very fact that I had asked for the appointment made him feel that I might be one of those persons who really wanted to know what his lectures were about and had come to him to fill in the details.

Shortly thereafter he invited me to his house. Later, he invited me to dinner, and I soon became a fairly close friend of the family. At that time he was married to his second wife. She had had two daughters by her first marriage. One was twelve and the other fourteen. The thing that impressed me about all three of the women in the household was their protective attitude toward Veblen. They felt that they had to protect him against something. I could not understand what it was, but it was evident that they were going to see to it that nothing happened to him. Gradually all three of them developed a sort of motherly attitude toward me. By the time the year ended I had a feeling that this attitude toward me was partly due to the fact that they felt that I, too, wanted to protect Veblen. But again I'm not quite certain what he was being protected against.

At the end of the first semester Veblen asked me to take over the job of reading the class term papers. Apparently he wanted to get out of reading what turned out to be boring.

Another thing about his home life that impressed me was that the girls and Mrs. Veblen took *The Theory of the Leisure Class* seriously. Their clothes were functional; there was no adornment. They were constantly criticizing other girls for the way they dressed. As a matter of fact, there were times that I felt they suspected me because my family owned an automobile, which back in those days was still a luxury. It did not seem quite right to them that a person close to Veblen should own an automobile. They took what Veblen had said seriously and adapted their lives to it. For example, I never knew either of the girls to go to a movie. As a matter of fact the only time I know of Veblen having gone to a movie was back in 1917. "The Birth of a Nation" was being shown at a local movie house, and I persuaded him to see it with me. We sat through the picture, which at that time was two and a half hours long. It was a silent film. Veblen, too, was silent throughout the showing. On the way home, in commenting on the film, he said, "Lubin, that is the finest example of concentrated misinformation that I've ever seen."

The Veblen home was very simple. Veblen was proud of several of the living room chairs that he had made. He dressed simply, usually wearing tweeds. Nevertheless, he had many so-called leisure class desires. He liked good food, not only at home but when we went out to dinner, which we used to do occasionally when he was living in New York. He always smoked a very expensive brand of Turkish cigarettes, a luxury he justified by insisting that the particular Turkish brand he smoked "was the only kind that was fit to smoke."

I was aware during my early days at Missouri that Veblen had very few close friends in Columbia. Although he had many admirers on the faculty, he had no close relationships with them. He rarely went out to visit or to dine with other people. When he was living in New York things were different. There he did have some very intimate friends. But at Missouri I rarely met anybody at his home except people who happened to be passing through the Middle West and wanted to see what Veblen looked like. This is not to say that Veblen was an aloof person. He had difficulty in making intimate friends, and I think this had much to do with the attitude of the family toward him. They felt that they had to make up for the things he did not get by association with other people.

It is interesting to note, also, that during my visits to the Veblen house and in the walks that we would take he rarely, if ever, discussed any of the problems of economic theory that were bothering him. But every now and then, if we were discussing some current happening, he would comment on it in terms of his economic philosophy.

Incidentally, he loved to walk around the university golf course, and he had an uncanny ability to find lost golf balls. I do not know whether he had a golf ball detector in his pocket, but he had a collection of hundreds of balls. They were his "trophies," which he liked to show off and boast about.

In addition to making me walk with him, he would occasionally put me to work doing chores. I remember most distinctly a tree in front of his house that he wanted chopped down. He gave me an axe, and I went to work. I had never handled an axe in my life, and I really made a mess of the tree. When he saw it, he said, "Lubin, I didn't ask you to manufacture toothpicks." He then took the axe himself and cut what was left into a neat stump, with a skill that only a woodsman could show.

From that moment on I began to question his occasional complaints about his health. I was never certain that he was the sickly person he wanted us to think he was. On many occasions I saw him carry heavy suitcases without any hesitation, without any strain, or any difficulty.

Veblen had a great love for Norway. Despite everything he said and wrote about patriotism and the self-aggrandizement of "the vested interests" in the name of patriotism, when it came to Norway he was as great a chauvinist as anybody I ever knew. When he talked about the country his face lit up. I used to chide him about his attitude toward Norway. I went there for the first time in 1929, and I wrote him a letter from Oslo in which I said that having been there I now agreed with his feelings about Norway and forgave him for being chauvinistic about the country. He died that week and never saw the letter. All of this is to say that Veblen was human. He had all the weaknesses that the rest of us have when it comes to things that are close to us.

Veblen did most of his writing in bed, sitting up with a couple of pillows behind him and a small bed table in front of him. He always wrote on yellow unruled paper and always with a pencil. This was true even when he was on *The Dial* editorial staff and had a secretary. As he once said to me: "I think through my fingers."

Regarding Veblen's economic philosophy, I think that I can honestly say that in all my contacts with him I never saw evidence of animus or personal dislike of the economic system

or of the people who ran the system. Veblen was not a reformer. Capitalism to him was a system which he was trying
to analyze as a scientist would analyze a rock of a certain
geologic age, or a doctor or a physiologist would analyze the
human body to see how it functioned. I never had the feeling
that he had an animus against the system; he was simply telling you what it was like and how it operated. I never heard
him express any hatred for a "captain of industry." Contrary
to what one might expect from reading his books, he had
nothing against the captains of industry whose operations he
was describing. At least I never had any evidence of it, either
in our conversations in class, around the house, or on our
many walks. As a matter of fact, despite everything he says
about the small businessman in the country town, he respected many of them. He respected them because some of
them did well by their customers through the quality of service they rendered and their personal interest. Indeed, he had
a respect for some small businessmen because they did not
take full advantage of the system under which they operated.
He had much respect for my father, who was a small businessman. The fact that my father had come here as a boy of
twelve from Lithuania and had moved up from a peddler to
owner of a successful business was an accomplishment that
impressed Veblen. He admired an individual who could accomplish this on his own without any association with the
banking fraternity or the "vested interests."

There were times when Veblen, in his writings, appeared
to be severely critical of certain financial and industrial leaders. He was not, however, criticizing them as individuals; he
was criticizing the environment in which they lived and in
which they acted. He made a distinction between the indi-

vidual as a human being and the individual as part of a mechanism, a way of life that prevailed in the economic arena.

Veblen, in other words, did not consider it his function to be a reformer. He looked upon himself rather as a social scientist whose job it was to analyze the functioning of our economic system. The system, as he saw it, was not, as the classical economists claimed, regulated by natural law.

Incidentally, there is a story about Veblen that I want to clear up. Dorfman, in his book, mentions the fact that Veblen's first wife had said that he did not know any English before he came to Carleton. This is very hard for me to believe. I remember his telling me, in discussing his mother, that only Norwegian was spoken in their household. When he was a youngster, he said, a peddler came to the house and rapped at the door. His mother got into an argument with the peddler, entirely in English. It was the first time in his life he had realized that his mother had a good command of the English language. He commented on the fact that she could not have handled herself so well if she had not known the English language very well. The very fact that he understood what she was saying convinces me that he knew English too. Although it may be true that he learned it in his teens, I have difficulty in believing that he did not know English until he was in college.

In January, 1918, I left Missouri to join the Food Administration in Washington. Shortly after arriving, I was asked whether Veblen might be interested in coming to the Food Administration. I said I thought that he would be. He arrived the next week and we had adjoining offices. Soon after he arrived a sign was put on Veblen's door: Dr. Thorstein B.

Veblen. His comment to me when he saw the sign was: "Get that goddam sign off of there. The only reason I came here was to get rid of the title Doctor."

We were located in one of those "temporary" buildings that had been erected in a hurry in Washington after the United States entered the war. It was newly built and was a whole block long. We had all kinds of messenger boys running around on rubber-wheeled roller skates. Veblen was fascinated by them. The messengers would rush by the door at twenty miles an hour. Veblen was very much impressed with it all and commented that his feeling that the Government was inefficient had to be changed.

The first job given to us was a study of the labor situation in the Northwest. With the slogan "Food Will Win the War" as the watchword of the day, the farmers were beginning to complain that their sons were being drafted, thereby limiting the farm labor supply needed to harvest their crops. Raymond Pearl, who was in charge of the Statistical Division, asked Veblen and me to go out to the wheat belt to see whether there was anything in the complaint and whether we could suggest ways to relieve the situation. We went first to Columbia, Missouri, where we spent several days talking to people in the Agricultural College there. We then went up to the Twin Cities and put up at the Faculty Club at the University. We had been there only a few days when Veblen developed a cold and went back to Columbia, Missouri, and I continued without him. At that time a significant number of the agricultural workers in this part of the country were members of the IWW—Industrial Workers of the World. They were in those days considered radicals. As a matter of fact, many of them had been indicted for interfering with the conduct of the war. They had called a strike in the Northwest which had caused great concern in Washington. It became apparent to Veblen and me that we ought to find out what was troubling these people. We might then appeal to them in some way and try to make them feel that they had a contribution to make toward winning the war.

After Veblen left, I began making inquiries as to how I could meet the leaders of the IWW in Minneapolis. I ran into a stone wall; nobody would give me any help. Those who knew the IWW leaders were afraid to talk to anybody from the government for fear of getting the leaders into trouble. By sheer chance I got a lead. An employee of the faculty club to whom I had been talking about the problem suggested that I see the mayor. I called the mayor's office, made an appointment, and went to see him. I told him my story and what I had in mind. He replied that he could help me to meet with the IWW leaders, but he insisted on a commitment from me that I would never reveal to his police department where the IWW officers were.

I went to see the leaders and they told me their grievances, some of which were quite legitimate. There was no doubt but that the agricultural workers were being exploited. They were migratory workers who moved North with the wheat crop. They complained about their living conditions, housing, and food, and their wages were not comparable to those of other workers in the nation. The one thing they tried hard to do was to convince me that they were not really as radical as people thought they were and that they were just as interested as anybody else in playing their part in winning the war. They went so far as to offer to commit themselves, if they received decent housing and a minimum wage, and the government ceased its prosecution, to harvest the grain crop with less waste than it ever had been harvested before, to see that every possible kernel of grain would be made available to the country. How serious they were, we never had an opportunity to find out.

I then went back to Columbia and wrote a report for Veblen covering what I had learned and what I had done. He elaborated on the report and submitted it to Herbert Hoover, the head of the Food Administration. On the surface the report was in no way radical or revolutionary. Veblen simply said that the IWW membership were being harassed by the government. He suggested that the harassment be stopped and that the IWW be given a chance to prove their loyalty to the government. His second suggestion was that since the IWW was suspicious of Mr. Burleson, the Secretary of Agriculture, who opposed the organization of agricultural labor, the task of producing food during the war be taken away from the Department of Agriculture and, like food conservation, be made the responsibility of the Food Administration. He suggested also that the Food Administration make an agreement with the IWW, giving it the job of harvesting the crop of the area, instead of having every farmer hire his own workers and worry whether there would be enough of them to harvest the grain. I might add, incidentally, that in 1950, when my fitness to hold the job of United States representative to the Economic and Social Conference at the United Nations was being looked into—this was at the height of the McCarthy days—it was interesting to find that this report on the IWW was one of the charges that was made against me. All that Veblen did was to suggest a simple way to solve the farm manpower problem in the Northwest. To him the answer was obvious. He was thinking only of the ultimate goal—getting more food to help win the war.

There was a similar situation in connection with a later memorandum that he wrote on the general shortage of manpower. We had reached the stage where the economy was getting to the bottom of the barrel of available manpower. It appeared that we might be headed for difficulty in filling the needs of the armed forces. (In the second World War we took care of our manpower needs more effectively through regulating the movement of workers from job to job with a view to getting them into employment that was essential to winning the war.) Veblen was asked to do some thinking about the general manpower shortage. In his memorandum on the subject he pointed out that the greatest amount of manpower at that moment "unproductive," as far as the war was concerned, was in retail distribution. He suggested that hundreds of thousands of people could be made available for waressential activities if our retail distribution system were reorganized. The retail distribution needs of our country, he added, could be met by the government's taking over the mailorder houses and tying them up with the parcel post and the express systems. If the government took over certain phases of retail distribution and used the mails for delivery, many more people would do their purchasing by mail order, with the result that there would be less need for country stores and stores in towns, thus making their employees available for war-essential work. It was a neat idea, but, in a democracy, when the government asks for a suggestion for solving a problem, we can hardly expect it to accept what would appear to be a revolutionary solution, and one which a large segment of the public would oppose. The retail section of our society is

very large, and every Congressman is interested in the vote of
the merchants in his community. Veblen did not give consideration to the political or social repercussions that his plan
involved. When faced with that fact, his answer was simple.
"That's not my business. That doesn't concern me. They
asked me what they might do and this is what I suggested
they do."

I cite these instances because they illustrate the fact that
Veblen felt it his function to show how the "business as
usual" approach was not conducive to solving the problems
that arise when we are engaged in a war. Only on rare occasions did he attempt to provide politically feasible solutions
to the problems of our economic system. He was not a Marx-
ist. He did not believe in the class struggle as the instrument
for adjusting our problems. He did, however, have a manner
of dissecting the economic system that led toward a precon-
ceived conclusion.

One further word on our experiences in the Food Administration. After we had submitted our IWW memorandum on
manpower, somehow or other everybody forgot that either
Lubin or Veblen worked for the Food Administration. It
became quite evident the Mr. Hoover did not have the
courage to tell us we were fired. The only thing we found
coming over our desks was our personal mail. There were no
memoranda, no requests for information or ideas. We concluded that we were no longer wanted. Veblen went up to his
camp in Wisconsin for the summer, and I went to work with
Wesley Mitchell at the War Industries Board.

One thing that interested me during the war period was
Veblen's deep concern over the Russian-German Peace
Treaty. Despite all of his criticisms of our economic system he

was greatly upset when the Russians made peace with the Germans. Here for the first time was a leftist government in power in a feudal country with the potentialities of making a marked contribution to the welfare of its people. Yet he was very much worried by it. He was convinced that the treaty was going to make it much more difficult for us to defeat Germany. This concern was particularly significant in view of his memorandum on *The Nature of Peace,* in which he stated that the prevailing price system was inimical to the maintenance of peace. In his opinion, the job that took precedence over every other job was the winning of the war. Anything that interfered with winning, even though it might in the future bring a better world, as he thought it might, seriously bothered him.

During my early association with Veblen I never had the feeling that he was a reformer. He was fundamentally an analyst. He was a scientist looking at a phenomenon and depicting how it operated. It was not until the early 1920s that he seemed to be trying to do something about the system he had been criticizing. I had this impression when he was writing *The Engineer and the Price System.* Even in that book he made no suggestions as to how to bring about the changes in the system that he felt were necessary. He merely said that we ought to turn the whole job over to a syndicate of engineers, since they have no vested interest in profit per se. Their main interest, as he saw it, was in getting things done. He did not face any of the significant problems that would have to be resolved if the engineers took over. For example, he did not deal with the ways the use of our resources would have to be determined, how decisions would be made as to what should be produced, and how much of various things should be produced. These are decisions that have to be made under any economic system, whether it be an individual-enterprise system or a Communist or Socialist system. He presented no substitute for the price system whose weaknesses he had been revealing. I think we shall all agree that the price system does not function perfectly as a determinant of the use of resources. However, even Communist countries like the Soviet Union, Poland, and Yugoslavia are now beginning to use profits and prices as a determinant of what shall be made. They are more and more letting the market decide what and how much shall be produced. If the market is receptive to what they produce, they produce more. If it is not, they change their output quotas.

To sum up, Veblen refused to accept the thesis of the classical economists that our economic system is based on "natural law." The system is not God made. Our institutions are man made and that being the case, man can change them. If man "created" the existing institutional situation, man ought to be able to adjust and change it.

Even though he rarely suggested specific changes, Veblen was convinced that our economic institutions could be changed by mobilizing political and social forces in our society. Indeed, I have always felt that it was his desire to mobilize these forces that accounted for the manner in which he presented his analysis of the economic system. But he always gave the impression, either in an aside or at the end of a paragraph or chapter, that certain forces in our society would not permit radical changes in our economic system.

Had Veblen lived through the 1930s and seen the accomplishments of that decade, I think he would have been less pessimistic as to what changes could be made in our economic and social institutions. He would have seen the establishment of the Securities and Exchange Commission, which regulates the issue of corporate securities and requires the publication of information bearing upon the financial structure of corporations. He would have witnessed the passage of the Minimum Wage Act, which imposes minimum wages and regulates hours of employment, and which was enacted despite the overwhelming opposition of the "vested interests." He would have seen a Social Security Act and an Unemployment Insurance Law put into effect. As was to be expected, the "vested interests" opposed these reforms, but despite their opposition social and political forces in the United States made these advances a reality.

And had Veblen been able to live in the 1960s he would have seen these institutions further implemented by the "War on Poverty" and the concept of "The Great Society." But much more significantly, Veblen would have seen the very people who had opposed changes in the existing order develop a vested interest in the maintenance of these social reforms. They have found that the billions paid out in unemployment insurance help maintain a steadier flow of demand for their products. They have found that the older people who formerly had to live on the largess of their families or public relief now have incomes to buy their goods and services. They have come to the conclusion that you cannot have a profitable market in a country made up of poor people with no incomes. In short, "vested interests" have learned that they have much to gain from the changes that Veblen said could not possibly be made because of their opposition.

What we have in effect been doing is creating a mass leisure class which is entirely different from the "leisure class"

that Veblen portrayed in his writings. The new leisure class is
not restricted to the upper few. Indeed, we are fast approaching the point in the United States where there will shortly be
more people enrolled in educational courses, private and public, than there will be people actually in the labor force. We
are in the process of creating a "learning" force. Our problem
now is to use our new leisure in a way that will permit the
individual to make the greatest possible contribution to society and to self-realization in the arts and the nonpecuniary
aspects of life. In other words, we have passed the stage where
leisure's function is to make it possible for one to spend as
much money as one wants on something that the other person
cannot have. During the last thirty years we have gone
through radical changes in our attitude toward life—changes
that Veblen could not anticipate because he did not think
they would be permitted by the "vested interest." These
changes are reflected in our favorable reactions to Mrs. Lyn-
don Johnson's program for cleaning up the roadsides, in the
current interest in making our cities more attractive and
livable, the trend toward the creation of new towns, and in
the development of local performing arts institutions.

Kenneth Galbraith, at a meeting on urban America that I
attended several months ago said: "We can't afford to give
priority to economic goods. We must assert the claims of the
community against the claims of economics." What he was
saying in effect was that in urban renewal our criterion is not
how much money a given investment will yield. Our criteria
should be human health, which is expensive. How much will
it improve our educational facilities? How much will it add
to esthetic living? How will it meet our needs for parks and
playgrounds? These are all things whose value is not measur-

able in pecuniary terms. In other words, we are shifting our system of values in determining priorities in our present society.

If I were to summarize what I have written I would say that I believe if Veblen were alive today, despite everything he wrote and said, he would be pleasantly disappointed with the developments that have taken place in our economic and social institutions during the last three and a half decades.

Notes

Introduction

1. Joseph Dorfman, *Thorstein Veblen and His America* (New York, Viking, 1935), p. 518.

2. Max Lerner, editor, *The Portable Veblen* (New York, Viking, 1948), p. 48.

3. Wesley C. Mitchell, editor, *What Veblen Taught* (New York, Viking, 1936), p. xlix.

4. Andrew Veblen to Joseph Dorfman, March 13, 1930. In Archives of the Norwegian-American Historical Association, Northfield, Minnesota.

5. *Ibid.*

6. Thorstein Veblen, translator and editor, *The Laxdaela Saga* (New York, Huebsch, 1925). A new translation by A. Margaret Arent was published by the University of Washington Press in 1964.

7. *Ibid.,* p. x.

8. "Memoirs of Emily Veblen." In Archives of Norwegian-American Historical Association, Northfield, Minnesota.

9. R. L. and William M. Duffus, *The Innocents at Cedro* (New York, Macmillan, 1944).

10. Douglas F. Dowd, *Thorstein Veblen* (New York, Washington Square Press, 1966).

11. The essays by the student members of the seminar are gratefully acknowledged in the preparation of Part II of this Introduction.

12. John Kenneth Galbraith, *The New Industrial State* (Boston, Houghton Mifflin, 1967), Chapter VI.

13. *Ibid.*

14. Adolf A. Berle and Gardner C. Means, *The Modern Corporation and Private Property* (New York, Macmillan, 1934); E. J. Lar-

ner, "The 200 Largest Nonfinancial Corporations" in *The American Economic Review*, LVI (September 1966), 777–87.

15. Galbraith, *The New Industrial State*.

Veblen on the Future of American Capitalism

1. Most of Veblen's methodological essays are collected in Thorstein Veblen, *The Place of Science in Modern Civilisation* (New York, Heubsch, 1919).

2. Joseph Dorfman, *Thorstein Veblen and His America* (New York, Viking, 1934), p. 311.

3. Veblen, "Why Is Economics Not an Evolutionary Science?," *The Place of Science in Modern Civilisation*, pp. 67–68.

4. Veblen, *The Theory of Business Enterprise* (New York, Scribner's, 1904), p. 377.

5. Clarence Ayres, *The Theory of Economic Progress* (Chapel Hill, University of North Carolina Press, 1944).

6. Veblen, *The Theory of Business Enterprise*, p. 77.

7. *Ibid.*, p. 77.   8. *Ibid.*, p. 77.   9. *Ibid.*, p. 35.

10. *Ibid.*, p. 271.   11. *Ibid.*, pp. 26–27.   12. *Ibid.*, p. 53.

13. See Charles B. Friday, "Veblen *versus* Chamberlin on Monopolistic Competition," *Proceedings* (Western Economic Association, 1954), pp. 54–57. For Chamberlin monopolistic competition became a concept used to explain a static problem in resource allocation. His equilibrium solution emphasized excess capacity and a higher than perfectly competitive price. Veblen reached the same conclusion without the geometrical apparatus that is so important to Chamberlin's model. His historical, evolutionary approach attempts to show the long-run consequences for capitalism of such monopolistic practices. It becomes a part of his theory of development.

14. Veblen, *The Theory of Business Enterprise*, pp. 54–55.

15. Veblen, *Absentee Ownership and Business Enterprise in Recent Times* (New York, Viking, 1933), p. 128.

16. Veblen, *The Theory of Business Enterprise*, p. 51.

17. *Ibid.*, p. 215.

18. See R. Vining, "Suggestions of Keynes in the Writings of Veblen," *Journal of Political Economy*, XLVII (October, 1939), pp. 692–

704, and M. D. Brockie, "The Cycle Theories of Veblen and Keynes Today," in *Thorstein Veblen: A Critical Reappraisal* edited by D. F. Dowd (Ithaca, Cornell University Press, 1958), pp. 113–28.

19. Veblen, *The Theory of Business Enterprise,* p. 234.

20. Veblen, *Absentee Ownership,* p. 112.

21. Veblen, *Imperial Germany and the Industrial Revolution* (Ann Arbor, University of Michigan Press, 1966), p. 33. Veblen appears to argue that the slack *is* taken up by private conspicuous consumption and waste. That failure to "take up the slack" may result in recession is nowhere clear in his analysis. Here again his lack of a theory of aggregate demand prevents his making his case for stagnation stronger than it already is.

22. Veblen, *The Vested Interests and the State of the Industrial Arts* (New York, Heubsch, 1919), p. 55. For enlightening comment on this concept, see Allan G. Grughy, "Veblen's Theory of Economic Growth," in Dowd (editor), *Thorstein Veblen,* pp. 151–76.

23. Veblen, *The Theory of Business Enterprise,* p. 64.

24. *Ibid.,* p. 284–85.   25. *Ibid.,* pp. 268–69.   26. *Ibid.,* p. 286.

27. *Ibid.,* p. 289.   28. *Ibid.,* p. 374.   29. *Ibid.,* p. 375.

30. *Ibid.,* p. 309.   31. *Ibid.,* p. 342.

32. Several of these essays are reprinted in Veblen, *Essays in Our Changing Order,* edited by Leon Ardzrooni (New York, Viking, 1934). See especially pp. 399 ff.

33. Veblen, *The Theory of Business Enterprise,* p. 292.

34. *Ibid.,* p. 391.   35. *Ibid.,* pp. 392–93.

36. *Ibid.,* pp. 297–98.   37. *Ibid.,* p. 395.   38. *Ibid.,* p. 301.

39. *Ibid.,* p. 376.   40. *Ibid.,* p. 400.

41. J. M. Keynes, *The General Theory of Employment, Interest, and Money* (New York, Harcourt, Brace, 1936), Chapter 24.

42. See B. H. Wilkins and C. B. Friday, *The Economists of the New Frontier* (New York, Random House, 1963), Introduction. Even such upholders of the Establishment as *Time* reports that "we are all Keynesians now" (December 31, 1965).

43. Forest G. Hill, "Veblen and Marx," in Dowd, p. 148.

44. Veblen, "The Socialist Economics of Karl Marx and His Followers," in *The Place of Science in Modern Civilisation,* p. 447.

45. Veblen, *The Theory of Business Enterprise,* p. 378.

46. Veblen, "Bolshevism Is a Menace—to Whom?," in *Essays in Our Changing Order,* p. 403.

47. Veblen, *The Theory of Business Enterprise,* p. 287.

48. J. K. Galbraith, *The Affluent Society* (Boston, Houghton Mifflin, 1958).

49. Veblen, *The Theory of the Leisure Class* (New York, Modern Library, 1934), p. 84.

50. *Ibid.,* pp. 336–37.

51. Clarence Ayres, *Toward a Reasonable Society* (Austin, University of Texas Press, 1961), p. 198.

52. Veblen, "Between Bolshevism and War," in *Essays in Our Changing Order,* p. 437.

53. Eugene McCarthy, "The U.S.: Supplier of Weapons to the World," *Saturday Review,* (July 9, 1966), pp. 13–15.

Business in Veblen's America

1. Veblen, *The Theory of Business Enterprise* (New York, Scribner's, 1904), p. 4.

2. See, for example: Thomas C. Cochran and others, "Historical Aspects of Imperfect Competition," *The Journal of Economic History, Supplement III* (1943), pp. 27–50; and Veblen, *Theory of Business Enterprise,* p. 54.

3. Thomas C. Cochran, *Basic History of American Business* (Princeton, N.J., Van Nostrand, Anvil Books, 1959), pp. 139–40.

4. Hans B. Thorelli, *The Federal Antitrust Policy* (Baltimore, Johns Hopkins University Press, 1955), pp. 77–80. Henry R. Seager and Charles A. Gulick, Jr., *Trust and Corporation Problems* (New York, Harper, 1929), p. 51.

5. Henry Demarest Lloyd, *Wealth against Commonwealth* (Englewood Cliffs, Prentice-Hall, Spectrum Books, 1963).

6. Cochran, *Basic History of American Business,* p. 72.

7. Morton Keller, *The Life Insurance Enterprise, 1885–1910* (Cambridge, Belknap Press, Harvard University Press, 1963), pp. 158–61.

8. Mark Sullivan, *Our Times,* (New York, Scribner's, 1927), Vol. II, p. 318.

9. *Historical Statistics of the United States* (Washington, Govern-

ment Printing Office) lumps trade, finance, and real estate together through 1900, and real estate and finance thereafter; see p. 74.

10. Otis Pease, *The Responsibilities of American Advertising* (New Haven, Yale University Press, 1958) , p. 13.

11. Merle Curti and Associates, *The Making of an American Community* (Stanford, Stanford University Press, 1959) , p. 223.

12. *Ibid.*, p. 227.

13. Cochran, *Railroad Leaders: The Business Mind in Action, 1845–1890* (Cambridge, Harvard University Press, 1953) , p. 445.

14. *Ibid.*, pp. 80–90.   15. *Ibid.*, p. 111–12.

16. *Ibid.*, p. 117.   17. *Ibid.*, p. 117.

18. *Ibid.*, p. 117.   19. *Ibid.*, p. 203.   20. *Ibid.*, p. 203.

21. *Ibid.*, p. 152.   22. *Ibid.*, p. 155.   23. *Ibid.*, p. 204.

24. *Ibid.*, p. 205.   25. *Ibid.*, p. 206.   26. *Ibid.*, p. 211.

27. *Ibid.*, p. 212.   28. *Ibid.*, p. 212   29. *Ibid.*, p. 205.

The Theology of Thorstein Veblen

1. David W. Noble, "The New Republic and the Idea of Progress," 1914–1920, *Mississippi Valley Historical Review*, Vol. 38, No. 3, (December, 1951) pp. 387–402.

2. Noble, *The Paradox of Progressive Thought* (Minneapolis, University of Minnesota Press, 1958) .

3. Mircea Eliade, *The Sacred and the Profane* (Harper, 1961) , pp. 72, 81, 82, 92.

4. *Ibid.*, p. 107.

5. Veblen, "Why Is Economics Not an Evolutionary Science," *Quarterly Journal of Economics*, XII (July, 1898) .

6. Veblen, "The Preconceptions of Economic Science," *Quarterly Journal of Economics*, XIII (January, 1899; July, 1899; February, 1900) .

7. Veblen, "The Socialist Economics of Karl Marx and His Followers," *Quarterly Journal of Economics*, XX (August, 1906) ; reprinted in *The Place of Science in Modern Civilisation* (New York, Huebsch, 1919) , p. 410.

8. *Ibid.*, pp. 417–18.

9. Veblen, *The Theory of the Leisure Class* (Macmillan, 1899), p. 24.

10. *Ibid.,* p. 58.   11. *Ibid.,* p. 133.   12. *Ibid.,* p. 162.

13. *Ibid.,* p. 145.   14. *Ibid.,* p. 148–49.   15. *Ibid.,* p. 217.

16. *Ibid.,* p. 233.   17. *Ibid.,* p. 248.

18. Veblen, *The Theory of Business Enterprise* (Scribner's, 1904), p. 13.

19. *Ibid.,* p. 151.   20. *Ibid.,* p. 134.   21. *Ibid.,* p. 147.

22. *Ibid.,* p. 177.   23. *Ibid.,* p. 169.

24. Veblen, *The Instinct of Workmanship* (New York, Macmillan, 1914), p. 36.

25. Veblen, "Christian Morals and the Competitive System," *International Journal of Ethics,* XX (January, 1910); reprinted in *Essays in Our Changing Order,* edited by Leon Ardzrooni (Viking, 1934), p. 209.

26. *Ibid.,* p. 218.

27. Veblen, *Imperial Germany and the Industrial Revolution,* (New York, Macmillan, 1915), p. 41.

28. *Ibid.,* p. 3.   29. *Ibid.,* p. 262.

30. Veblen, *The Vested Interests* (New York, Huebsch, 1919), p. 10.

31. Veblen, *The Engineers and the Price System* (New York, Huebsch, 1921), p. 80.

32. *Ibid.,* p. 52.

33. Veblen, *The Vested Interests,* pp. 140–41; *The Engineers and the Price System,* p. 134.

34. Veblen, *The Engineers and the Price System,* pp. 136–37.

35. *Ibid.,* p. 159.   36. *Ibid.,* p. 57.

Background of Veblen's Thought

1. Andrew Veblen was also a graduate of Carleton and was the father of the famous mathematician Oswald Veblen.

2. Thorstein Veblen to Andrew Veblen in the fall of 1928, quoted by Andrew Veblen in a letter to "Emily, May and Hannah," April 9, 1931, Manuscript Division of the Minnesota Historical Society. The sister-in-law was the wife of his brother Orson. The remainder of the quoted part reads, "And by the way, it is not quite true that

I consented to her asking or getting any material you may have unless silence gives consent. She asked me and I neglected to answer the question, though I did not refuse leave to write about me. She had a sort of claim on my good will just then, in that she (or her sister) had just paid up the mortgage (of $2,500) given by Orson which I held on her home, in full, and it would not make any difference anyway. Also I don't see there is anything to write about."

3. Mitchell, "James Harvey Robinson," memorial meeting, New School for Social Research, April 16, 1936, in Special Collections, Columbia University Libraries. Robinson was a pioneer in the United States in transforming the study of history into cultural history. Professor Mitchell, in his memorial address, stated that "one trait of Robinson's that especially endeared him to me was his warm admiration of Thorstein Veblen. Not many men of Robinson's antecedents had the open-mindedness to understand Veblen's quizzical critique of modern culture."

4. J. M. Clark, "Thorstein Bunde Veblen: 1857–1929," *The American Economic Review* (1929), p. 742.

5. Veblen to J. Franklin Jameson, February 12, 1883, in Jameson Papers, Library of Congress, printed in Joseph Dorfman, *Thorstein Veblen and His America* (1934), 7th ed. (New York, Kelley, 1965), p. 544. Jameson became a leading American historian. The editors of his correspondence have noted: "Proud of his New England birth and scornful of anything 'westernish,' he [Jameson] was yet able to recognize the unusual powers of Thorstein Veblen, a fellow student [at Johns Hopkins]." *An Historian's World: Selections from the Correspondence of John Franklin Jameson,* edited by Elizabeth Donnan and L. F. Stock (Philadelphia, The American Philosophical Society, 1956), p. 2.

6. Veblen especially appreciated Sumner's two-year course on the political and financial history of the United States.

7. Ellen Rolfe's father, Charles Rolfe, was a member of the Kansas City Board of Trade and held substantial interests in grain elevators. The president of the college, the Reverend James W. Strong, was her uncle. Another uncle, William Barstow Strong, was the president of the Atchison, Topeka, and Santa Fe Railroad.

8. Clark, "Thorstein Bunde Veblen: 1857–1929," p. 742.

9. The first four Veblen essays appeared in the Harvard-edited

The *Quarterly Journal of Economics* and the last appeared in *The Publications of the American Economic Association.* All are reprinted in Veblen's *The Place of Science in Modern Civilization and Other Essays* (1919), 5th ed. (New York, Russell & Russell, 1961), with a preface by Joseph Dorfman, pp. 56–179, 279–323.

10. A. L. Perry, *Elements of Political Economy* (New York, Scribner's, 1868), p. 123.

11. The Reverend Charles Beard, *The Universal Christ,* in Joseph Dorfman, "Modern Reform and the Reformation," foreword to new edition of Beard, *The Reformation of the 16th Century* (Ann Arbor, University of Michigan Press, 1962), p. xiii.

12. An extreme presentation of the Spencerian view was given by an Australian economist in 1876: "The data of political economy —the laws of the pressure of population, of demand and supply, of natural selection and the survival of the fittest—are simply impregnable inductions from the phenomena of nature and of human society. . . . The survival of the fittest means that might, wisely used, is right. And thus we invoke, and remorselessly fulfill, the inexorable law of natural selection (or of demand and supply) when exterminating the inferior Australian and Maori races (savages), and we appropriate their patrimony as coolly as Ahab did the vineyard of Naboth." H. K. Rusden, "Labour and Capital," *Melbourne Review,* January, 1876, pp. 69, 82.

13. "If the organization and improvement of government and of all other human institutions as well as the operation of the various civilizing agencies of mankind are normal products of evolution and have taken place under the operation of natural laws, made possible only through the existence of the intellectual faculty of man, . . . what is there in the world that can be called artificial?" Lester F. Ward, *The Psychic Factors of Civilization* (Boston, Ginn, 1893), p. 286.

14. *Dynamic Sociology,* 2 vols. (New York, Appleton, 1883), p. 131.

15. Veblen's trips to Europe and in particular to Scandinavia were largely to study northern antiquities and ethnographic material. (Veblen to Andrew Veblen, August 16, 1899, Andrew Veblen Papers, Minnesota Historical Society.)

16. Boas, "The Social Organization and the Secret Societies of the Kwakiutl Indians," *Annual Report of the Board of Regents of the Smithsonian Institution* (1895), part 2, p. 343; Boas, "First General Report on the Indians of British Columbia," *Report of the Fifty-Ninth Meeting of the British Association for the Advancement of Science* (1899), p. 834.

17. Dewey, review of L. F. Ward, "The Psychic Factors of Civilization," *Psychological Review* (July 1894), p. 405.

18. The quotation is from the summary of Dewey's psychology by George H. Mead, "The Definition of the Psychical," *The Decennial Publications of the University of Chicago* (Chicago, University of Chicago Press, 1903), first series, III, 98.

19. "Minutes of the Trustees," copy in Columbiana Collection, Columbia University Libraries.

20. Adams to E.R.A. Seligman, June 20, 1887, "The Seligman Correspondence," no. 2, edited by Joseph Dorfman, *Political Science Quarterly* (June 1941), p. 271.

21. "General overproduction," in Mr. Wells' use, means a general production in excess of the "demand at remunerative prices." Veblen, "The Overproduction Fallacy," 1892; reprinted in *Essays in Our Changing Order,* edited by Leon Ardzooni (New York, Viking, 1934), p. 109.

22. *Recent Economic Changes* (New York, Appleton, 1889), p. 75.

23. W. C. Mitchell, "Fifty Years as an Economist," talk to Economics Club, Columbia University, May 11, 1945, in Mitchell Papers.

24. L. B. Johnson, "The State of the Union," *The Congressional Record* (January 4, 1965), 27, 28; "The Economic Report," *The Congressional Record* (January 28, 1965), 1403, 1404, 1407.

Writings of Thorstein Veblen

1882. "J. S. Mill's Theory of the Taxation of Land," Johns Hopkins University, *University Circulars,* Feb., p. 176.

1884. "Kant's Critique of Judgment," [1] *Journal of Speculative Philosophy,* July, pp. 260–274.

1891. "Some Neglected Points in the Theory of Socialism," [2] *Annals of the American Academy of Political and Social Science,* Nov., pp. 345–362.

1892. "Böhm-Bawerk's Definition of Capital and the Source of Wages," [1] *Quarterly Journal of Economics,* Jan., pp. 247–252.

"The Overproduction Fallacy," [1] *Quarterly Journal of Economics,* July, pp. 484–492.

"The Price of Wheat Since 1867," *Journal of Political Economy,* Dec., pp. 68–103 and appendix pp. 156–161.

1893. Review of Thomas Kirkup's *A History of Socialism,* in *Journal of Political Economy,* March, pp. 300–302.

Review of Otto Warschauer's *Geschichte des Socialismus und Communismus im 19. Jahrhundert,* in *Journal of Political Economy,* March, p. 302.

"The Food Supply and the Price of Wheat," *Journal of Political Economy,* June, pp. 365–379.

Review of B. H. Baden-Powell's *The Land-Systems of British India,* in *Journal of Political Economy,* Dec., pp. 112–115.

From the Augustus M. Kelley "Reprints of Economic Classic," 1966 edition of Joseph Dorfman's *Thorstein Veblen and His America,* pp. 519–24. Reprinted here by permission of August M. Kelley Publishers.

1 Republished in *Essays in Our Changing Order.*

2 Republished in *Place of Science in Modern Civilisation and Other Essays.*

1894. Review of Karl Kautsky's *Der Parlamentarismus und die Volksgesetzgebung und die Socialdemokratie,* in *Journal of Political Economy,* March, pp. 312–314.

Review of William E. Bear's *A Study of Small Holdings,* in *Journal of Political Economy,* March, pp. 325–326.

"The Army of the Commonweal," [1] *Journal of Political Economy,* June, pp. 456–461.

Review of Joseph Stammhammer's *Bibliographie des Socialismus und Communismus,* in *Journal of Political Economy,* June, pp. 474–475.

Review of Russell M. Garnier's *History of the English Landed Interest (Modern Period),* in *Journal of Political Economy,* June, pp. 475–477.

Review of Émile Levasseur's "L'Agriculture aux États-Unis," in *Journal of Political Economy,* Aug., pp. 592–596.

"The Economic Theory of Woman's Dress," [1] *Popular Science Monthly,* Nov., pp. 198–205.

1895. Review of Robert Flint's *Socialism,* in *Journal of Political Economy,* March, pp. 247–252.

The Science of Finance, translation of Gustav Cohn's *System der Finanzwissenschaft.*

1896. Review of Karl Marx's *Misère de la Philosophie,* in *Journal of Political Economy,* Dec., pp. 97–98.

Review of Enrico Ferri's *Socialisme et Science Positive,* in *Journal of Political Economy,* Dec., pp. 98–103.

1897. Review of Richard Calwer's *Einführung in den Socialismus,* in *Journal of Political Economy,* March, pp. 270–272.

Review of G. de Molinari's *La Viriculture—Ralentissement de la Population—Dégénérescence—Causes et Remèdes,* in *Journal of Political Economy,* March, pp. 273–275.

Review of Antonio Labriola's *Essais sur la conception matérialiste de l'histoire,* in *Journal of Political Economy,* June, pp. 390–391.

Review of Werner Sombart's *Sozialismus und soziale Bewegung im 19. Jahrhundert,* in *Journal of Political Economy,* June, pp. 391–392.

[1] Republished in *Essays in Our Changing Order.*

Review of N. Ch. Bunge's *Esquisses de littérature politico-économique,* in *Journal of Political Economy,* Dec., pp. 126–128.

Review of Max Lorenz's *Die Marxistische Socialdemokratie,* in *Journal of Political Economy,* Dec., pp. 136–137.

1898. Review of Gustav Schmoller's *Über einige Grundfragen der Socialpolitik und der Volkswirtschaftslehre,* in *Journal of Political Economy,* June, pp. 416–419.

Review of William H. Mallock's *Aristocracy and Evolution: A Study of the Rights, the Origin and the Social Functions of the Wealthier Classes,* in *Journal of Political Economy,* June, pp. 430–435.

"Why Is Economics Not an Evolutionary Science?" 2 *Quarterly Journal of Economics,* July, pp. 373–397.

"The Instinct of Workmanship and the Irksomeness of Labour," 1 *American Journal of Sociology,* Sept., pp. 187–201.

Review of Turgot, *Reflections on the Formation and the Distribution of Riches,* in *Journal of Political Economy,* Sept., pp. 575–576.

"The Beginnings of Ownership," 1 *American Journal of Sociology,* Nov., pp. 352–365.

"The Barbarian Status of Women," 1 *American Journal of Sociology,* Jan., pp. 503–514.

1899. *The Theory of the Leisure Class: an Economic Study of the Evolution of Institutions;* title changed in 1912 to *The Theory of the Leisure Class: an Economic Study of Institutions.*

"The Preconceptions of Economic Science," 2 *Quarterly Journal of Economics,* Jan., pp. 121–150; July, pp. 396–426; Jan., 1900, pp. 240–269.

Review of Simon Patten's *Development of English Thought,* in *Annals of the American Academy of Political and Social Science,* July, pp. 125–131.

"Mr. Cummings's Strictures on *The Theory of the Leisure Class,*" 1 *Journal of Political Economy,* Dec., pp. 106–117.

1 Republished in *Essays in Our Changing Order.*
2 Republished in *Place of Science in Modern Civilisation and Other Essays.*

1900. Review of Sir William Crooks' *The Wheat Problem, Revised, with an Answer to Various Critics,* in *Journal of Political Economy,* March, pp. 284–286.

Review of Arnold Fischer's *Die Entstehung des socialen Problems,* in *Journal of Political Economy,* March, pp. 286–287.

Review of Paul Lafargue's *Pamphlets socialistes: Le droit à la paresse; La religion du capital; L'appetit vendu; Pie IX au paradis,* in *Journal of Political Economy,* March, pp. 287–288.

Review of G. Tarde's *Social Laws; An Outline of Sociology,* in *Journal of Political Economy,* Sept., pp. 562–563.

Review of Basil A. Bauroff's *The Impending Crisis; Conditions Resulting from the Concentration of Wealth in the United States,* in *Journal of Political Economy,* Dec., pp. 159–160.

"Industrial and Pecuniary Employments," 2 *Publications of the American Economic Association,* Series 3, 1901, pp. 190–235.

1901. *Science and the Workingmen,* a translation of *Die Wissenschaft und die Arbeiter* by Ferdinand Lassalle, republished by German Publication Society in *The German Classics,* 1914, vol. 10.

"Gustav Schmoller's Economics," 2 *Quarterly Journal of Economics,* Nov., pp. 69–93.

1902. "Arts and Crafts," 1 *Journal of Political Economy,* Dec., pp. 108–111.

Review of Jules Gernaert's and Vte. de Herbais de Thun's *Associations industrielles et commerciales: Fédérations—Ententes partielles—Syndicats—Cartels—Comptoirs—Affiliations —Trusts,* in *Journal of Political Economy,* Dec., pp. 130–131.

Review of G. Tarde's *Psychologie économique,* in *Journal of Political Economy,* Dec., pp. 146–148.

1903. "The Use of Loan Credit in Modern Business," *Decennial Publications of the University of Chicago,* Series I, No. 4, pp.

---

1 Republished in *Essays in Our Changing Order.*

2 Republished in *Place of Science in Modern Civilisation and Other Essays.*

31–50, republished without substantial change in *The Theory of Business Enterprise.*

Review of Werner Sombart's *Der moderne Kapitalismus,* in *Journal of Political Economy,* March, pp. 300–305.

Review of T. H. Aschehoug's *Værdi—og Prillærens Historie,* in *Journal of Political Economy,* March, p. 306.

Review of Maurice Lair's *L'Impérialisme allemand,* in *Journal of Political Economy,* March, p. 306.

Review of J. A. Hobson's *Imperialism: a Study,* in *Journal of Political Economy,* March, pp. 311–319.

Review of Brooks Adams's *The New Empire,* in *Journal of Political Economy,* March, pp. 314–315.

Review of Theodore E. Burton's *Financial Crises and Periods of Industrial and Commercial Depression,* in *Journal of Political Economy,* March, pp. 324–326.

Review of Lester F. Ward's *Pure Sociology: a Treatise Concerning the Origin and Spontaneous Development of Society,* in *Journal of Political Economy,* Sept., pp. 655–656.

Review of Ludwig Pohle's *Bevölkerungsbewegung, Kapitalbildung und periodische Wirtschaftskrisen,* in *Journal of Political Economy,* Sept., pp. 656–657.

Review of S. Tschierschky's *Kartell und Trust: Vergleichende Untersuchungen über dem Wesen und Bedeutung,* in *Journal of Political Economy,* Sept., pp. 657–658.

1904. "An Early Experiment in Trusts," [2] *Journal of Political Economy,* March, pp. 270–279.

The Theory of Business Enterprise.

Review of Adam Smith's *An Inquiry into the Nature and Causes of the Wealth of the Nations,* in *Journal of Political Economy,* Dec., p. 136.

Review of Francis W. Hirst's *Adam Smith,* in *Journal of Political Economy,* Dec., pp. 136–137.

Review of Jacob Streider's *Zur Genesis des modernen Kapitalismus,* in *Journal of Political Economy,* Dec., pp. 120–122.

[2] Republished in *Place of Science in Modern Civilisation and Other Essays.*

1905. Review of Robert Francis Harper's *The Code of Hammurabi, King of Babylon about 2250 B.C.*, in *Journal of Political Economy*, March, pp. 319–320.

"Credit and Prices," [1] *Journal of Political Economy*, June, pp. 460–472.

1906. "The Place of Science in Modern Civilisation," [2] *American Journal of Sociology*, March, pp. 585–609.

"Professor Clark's Economics," [2] *Quarterly Journal of Economics*, Feb., pp. 147–195.

"Socialist Economics of Karl Marx and His Followers," [2] *Quarterly Journal of Economics*, Aug., pp. 578–595; Feb. 1907, pp. 299–322.

1907. Review of Sidney A. Reeve's *The Cost of Competition, An Effort at the Understanding of Familiar Facts*, in *Yale Review*, May, pp. 92–95.

"Fisher's Capital and Income," [1] *Political Science Quarterly*, March, pp. 112–128.

1908. "The Evolution of the Scientific Point of View," [2] *University of California Chronicle*, May, pp. 396–416.

"On the Nature of Capital," [2] *Quarterly Journal of Economics*, Aug., pp. 517–542; Nov., pp. 104–136.

1909. "Fisher's Rate of Interest," [1] *Political Science Quarterly*, June, pp. 296–303.

Review of Albert Schatz's *L'individualisme économique et sociale: ses origines—son évolution—ses formes contemporaires*, in *Journal of Political Economy*, June, pp. 378–379.

"The Limitations of Marginal Utility," [2] *Journal of Political Economy*, Nov., pp. 620–636.

1910. "Christian Morals and the Competitive System," [1] *International Journal of Ethics*, Jan., pp. 168–185.

"As to a Proposed Inquiry into Baltic and Cretan Antiquities," memorandum submitted to Carnegie Institution of Washington, published in *American Journal of Sociology*, Sept. 1933, pp. 237–241.

[1] Republished in *Essays in Our Changing Order*.
[2] Republished in *Place of Science in Modern Civilisation and Other Essays*.

"The Mutation Theory, the Blond Race, and the Aryan Culture," paper submitted to Carnegie Institution of Washington and later elaborated into the two papers following:

1913. "The Mutation Theory and the Blond Race," 2 *Journal of Race Development*, April, pp. 491–507.
"The Blond Race and the Aryan Culture," 2 *University of Missouri Bulletin, Science Series*, Vol. 2, No. 3, April, pp. 39–57.

1914. *The Instinct of Workmanship and the State of the Industrial Arts.*

1915. "The Opportunity of Japan," 1 *Journal of Race Development*, July, pp. 23–38; Review of Werner Sombart's *Der Bourgeois: zur Geistesgeschichte des modernen Wirtschaftsmenschen* in *Journal of Political Economy*, Oct., pp. 846–848.
Imperial Germany and the Industrial Revolution.

1916. Review of Maurice Millioud's *The Ruling Caste and Frenzied Trade in Germany*, in *Journal of Political Economy*, Dec., pp. 1019–1020.

1917. "Another German Apologist," review of *England, Its Political Organisation and Development and the War Against Germany*, by Eduard Meyer in *Dial*, April 19, pp. 344–345.
An Inquiry into the Nature of Peace and the Terms of its Perpetuation.
"The Japanese Lose Hopes for Germany," 1 letter to *New Republic*, June 30, pp. 246–247.
"Suggestions Touching the Working Program of an Inquiry into the Prospective Terms of Peace," 1 memorandum submitted to the House Inquiry, through Walter Lippmann, Dec., published in *Political Science Quarterly*, June 1932, pp. 186–189.
"An Outline of a Policy for the Control of the 'Economic Penetration' of Backward Countries and of Foreign Investments," 1 memorandum for House Inquiry published in *Political Science Quarterly*, June 1932, pp. 189–203.

---

1 Republished in *Essays in Our Changing Order.*
2 Republished in *Place of Science in Modern Civilisation and Other Essays.*

1918. "On the General Principles of a Policy of Reconstruction," *Journal of the National Institute of Social Sciences,* April, pp. 37–46; republished in part as:

"A Policy of Reconstruction," [1] *New Republic,* April 13, pp. 318–320. Report ad interim to Raymond Pearl on trip through prairie states in behalf of statistical division of Food Administration published in *American Economic Review,* Sept. 1933, pp. 478–479.

"Passing of National Frontiers," [1] *Dial,* April 25, pp. 387–390.

"Using the I.W.W. to Harvest Grain," [1] memorandum for Statistical Division of Food Administration, published in *Journal of Political Economy,* Dec. 1932, pp. 796–807.

"A Schedule of Prices for the Staple Foodstuffs," [1] memorandum for Statistical Division of Food Administration, published in *Southwestern Social Science Quarterly,* March, 1933, pp. 372–377.

"Menial Servants during the Period of the War," [1] *Public,* May 11, pp. 595–599.

"The War and Higher Learning," [1] *Dial,* July 18, pp. 45–49.

The Higher Learning in America, A Memorandum on the Conduct of Universities by Business Men.

"Farm Labour and the Country Towns," memorandum for the Statistical Division of the Food Administration and published in an elaborated form as:

"Farm Labour for the Period of the War," [1] *Public,* July 13, pp. 882–885; July 20, pp. 918–922; July 27, pp. 947–952; Aug. 3, pp. 981–985.

"The Modern Point of View and the New Order," *Dial,* Oct. 19, pp. 289–293; Nov. 2, pp. 349–354; Nov. 16, pp. 409–414; Nov. 30, pp. 482–488; Dec. 14, pp. 543–549; Dec. 28, pp. 605–611; Jan. 11, 1919; pp. 19–24; Jan. 25, pp. 75–82. Republished as:

1919. *The Vested Interests and the State of the Industrial Arts;* title changed in 1920 to *The Vested Interests and the Common Man.*

[1] Republished in *Essays in Our Changing Order.*

"Bolshevism Is a Menace—to Whom?" [1] *Dial,* Feb. 22, pp. 174-179.

"The Intellectual Pre-eminence of Jews in Modern Europe," [1] *Political Science Quarterly,* March, pp. 33-42.

"On the Nature and Uses of Sabotage," [3] *Dial,* April 5, pp. 341-346.

"Bolshevism Is a Menace to the Vested Interests," editorial, *Dial,* April 5, pp. 360-361.

"Sabotage," editorial, *Dial,* April 5, p. 363.

"Congressional Sabotage," editorial, *Dial,* April 5, p. 363.

"Immanuel Kant on Perpetual Peace," [1] editorial, *Dial,* May 3, p. 469.

"Peace," [1] *Dial,* May 17, pp. 485-487.

"The Captains of Finance and the Engineers," [3] *Dial,* June 14, pp. 599-606.

"Panem et Circenses," [1] editorial, *Dial,* June 14, p. 609.

"The Industrial System and the Captains of Industry," [3] *Dial,* May 31, pp. 552-557.

" 'Open Covenants Openly Arrived At' [1] and the Elder Statesmen," editorial, *Dial,* July 12, pp. 25-26.

"A World Safe for the Vested Interests," [1] editorial, *Dial,* July 12, p. 26.

"The Red Terror—At Last It Has Come to America," editorial, *Dial,* Sept. 6, p. 205.

"The Red Terror and the Vested Interests," editorial, *Dial,* Sept. 6, p. 206.

"Bolshevism and the Vested Interests in America," [3] *Dial,* Oct. 4, pp. 296-301; Oct. 18, 339-346; Nov. 1, 323-380.

"The Twilight Peace of the Armistice," [1] editorial, *Dial,* Nov. 15, p. 443.

The Place of Science in Modern Civilisation and Other Essays.

1920. Review of Keynes's *Economic Consequences of the Peace,*[1] in *Political Science Quarterly,* Sept., pp. 467-472.

[1] Republished in *Essays in Our Changing Order.*
[3] Republished in *The Engineers and the Price System.*

"Wire Barrage," memorandum printed in second edition of *Essays in Our Changing Order* (1964).

1921. *The Engineers and the Price System.*

"Between Bolshevism and War," [1] *Freeman,* May 25, pp. 248–251.

1922. "Dementia Præcox," [1] *Freeman,* June 21, pp. 344–347.

1923. "The Captain of Industry," [4] *Freeman,* April 18, pp. 127–132.

"The Timber Lands and Oil Fields," [4] *Freeman,* May 23, pp. 248–250; May 30, pp. 272–274.

"The Independent Farmer," [4] *Freeman,* June 13, pp. 321–324.

"The Country Town," [4] *Freeman,* July 11, pp. 417–420; July 18, pp. 440–443.

Absentee Ownership and Business Enterprise in Recent Times; the Case of America.

1925. "Economic Theory in the Calculable Future," [1] *American Economic Review,* March, Supplement, pp. 48–55.

The Laxdæla Saga, translated from the Icelandic with an Introduction.

1927. "An Experiment in Eugenics," published for the first time in *Essays in Our Changing Order.*

[1] Republished in *Essays in Our Changing Order.*

[4] Republished in *Absentee Ownership and Business Enterprise in Recent Times; The Case of America.*

Contributors

Charles B. Friday

Professor of Economics, Oregon State University. Co-editor, *The Economists of the New Frontier* (New York, Random House, 1963).

Thomas C. Cochran

Professor of History, University of Pennsylvania. Author, *The American Business System* (Cambridge, Harvard University Press, 1957), *The Age of Enterprise,* with William Miller (New York, Macmillan, 1942), and *Basic History of American Business* (Princeton, Van Nostrand, 1959).

David W. Noble

Professor of History, University of Minnesota. Author, *The Paradox of Progressive Thought* (Minneapolis, University of Minnesota Press, 1958) and *Historians against History* (Minneapolis, University of Minnesota Press, 1965).

Joseph Dorfman

Professor of Economics, Columbia University. Author, *Thorstein Veblen and His America* (New York, Viking, 1935; reprint edition, New York, Augustus M. Kelley, 1966); and *The Economic Mind in American Civilization* (New York, Viking, 1946–1959), 5 vols.

Isador Lubin

The Twentieth Century Fund, New York City. Economist and consultant to labor, business, and government. Close associate of Thorstein Veblen. Co-author, *Our Stake in World Trade* (New York, Foreign Policy Association, 1954).

Carlton C. Qualey

Editor of the present book. Laird Bell Professor of History, Carleton College. Author, *Norwegian Settlement in the United States* (Northfield, Norwegian-American Historical Association, 1938) ; contributor, *Immigration and American History,* edited by Henry Steele Commager (Minneapolis, University of Minnesota Press, 1961) .